Ten Ohio Disasters

ALSO BY NEIL ZURCHER

The Best of One Tank Trips
Tales from the Road
Strange Tales from Ohio
Ohio Oddities

Ten Ohio Disasters

*Stories of Tragedy and Courage
that Should Not Be Forgotten*

Neil Zurcher

Gray & Company, Publishers
Cleveland

Gray & Company, Publishers
www.grayco.com

ISBN 978-1-59851-125-3
Printed in the United States of America
1

Contents

This book is dedicated to my wife, Bonnie,
and to our first great-grandchild,
Kilian Ernest Justice.

Author's Note

IN WRITING THIS book I relied on multiple sources: my own recollections from covering events as a news reporter at the time; newspaper articles published immediately after the events; a few retrospective articles, videos, and books published years later; and new interviews with eyewitnesses that I conducted recently. Direct quotations from specific sources are attributed except for my own interviews, which are indicated by introducing them with the present tense: "So-and-so recalls . . ."

Journalism is called "the first draft of history," and as with any first draft, old newspaper stories sometimes contain errors, especially when they reported dramatic, chaotic, fast-breaking news. It's also true that many years after an event, the memories of eyewitnesses could sometimes be imperfect. (Although I was amazed at how clearly people remembered details of these life-changing tragedies.) Where I encountered differing statements of fact among sources, I tried to determine which seemed more reliable, or I presented both.

Sources that were particularly useful are listed by chapter at the end of this book.

One style note: The television station I worked for in Cleveland from 1962 to 2017 changed its call letters from WJW-TV to WJKW-TV and back again during that time. It also goes by Fox8 TV. In this book, for simplicity's sake, I refer to it as WJW-TV throughout.

Preface

I NOTICED IN a conversation with a friend a while back that stories that had once grabbed headlines across the country were slowly fading into the dust of history. Some of these stories I covered as a reporter. Others I did not report on but followed in the news like everyone else. As a journalist still, I was interested in learning more about these stories.

That's why I decided to write this book.

What I did not expect was that in the process I would discover heroes, meet some of the most fascinating people, and learn that even in the worst tragedy good things can happen.

When it comes to heroes, it's hard to beat the story of Ohio state patrolman Gary Taylor. During a killer tornado, while trying to reach his wife and children, he stopped in the middle of the storm to break up a robbery and care for an unconscious man. Then there is the tale of courage portrayed by Bob Coy of Springfield, who survived a parachute disaster over Lake Erie that killed sixteen of his friends. Chester Koch, a World War I veteran and civic-minded Cleveland citizen, with no special training or experience, ran into a city street to stop a runaway herd of elephants. Cincinnati broadcasting legend John London early in his career trudged seven miles on foot through the worst blizzard of the century to report on that storm. Elaine French and her young husband, Cliff, stopped in the middle of the night to assist at what turned out to be the worst nursing home fire in

American history. Sam Kopchak calmly led his horse away from a fully grown African lion that was stalking them in Zanesville. These are just a few of the heroes that I got to meet and write about in this book.

The legendary radio reporter Paul Harvey had a familiar catchphrase: "Now you know (long pause) . . . the rest of the story." Harvey would frequently end his radio show by retelling some big, well-known news event, then updating what had happened to the major players in those stories after the cameras had gone and the reporters had lost interest. Harvey showed that there was often more to the story—even a story widely reported at one time—if you kept looking. That is what I have tried to do in this book: retell some almost forgotten history and also share "the rest of the story."

Ten Ohio Disasters

The Parachute Disaster on Lake Erie

IT WAS SUNDAY, August 27, 1967, shortly after 4 p.m. on a breezy afternoon. Lt. Paul Potter of the United States Coast Guard was enjoying a day off on a beach near Huron, Ohio. He was gazing at Lake Erie, professionally noting that the waves were running about two to four feet, when an object high above the choppy waters caught his eye. At the base of a layer of rain clouds a parachute suddenly blossomed. Then another, and another, followed by even more.

Potter immediately realized that the parachutists were headed toward the water—and they were going to be in trouble when they hit it. He started running, frantically seeking a telephone so he could alert the Coast Guard Station in Lorain.

Where had the parachutists come from?

Later, in testimony in a federal court trial, it was learned that word had been circulating for weeks among local parachute clubs around the state that a high-altitude jump was being planned for that day at Ortner Airport near Birmingham, Ohio.

Bob Karns owned a vintage B-25 bomber, which he kept at Ortner Airport. Earlier that summer he had flown the plane at an air show and, as an added attraction, had invited some skydivers to jump from it at a later date. Karns had been paid for that performance, and now as a sort of thank you he was offering skydivers a free jump.

On the day of the jump, more skydivers showed up than had been expected. It was clear that not everyone would fit into the aircraft, so it was decided that only twenty skydivers would make the trip along with pilot Bob Karns and his copilot, Richard Wolfe. Eighteen would jump at 20,000 feet. The two most experienced skydivers would make their jump when the plane reached 30,000 feet.

Once it had finally been sorted out which twenty would go aloft and who would be left behind on the ground, parachutists filed aboard the aircraft.

The B-25 was a medium-range bomber used in World War II. Colonel Jimmy Doolittle had selected B-25s for his raid on Tokyo in 1942. Sixteen of them had taken off from the US aircraft carrier *Hornet* and struck the capital of the Empire of Japan.

In 1967, Karns's B-25, tail number N3443G, was still in its original bomber configuration. The plane had not been modified to carry sports parachutists, and with twenty of those on board, it would be crowded.

One of those boarding was Robert Coy, 29, of Springfield, Ohio. He was a highly experienced jumper, but this was going to be his first jump in more than a month. He had sprained his ankle six weeks earlier during a jump into a friend's wedding reception to deliver a large bottle of champagne. For this flight, Coy carried with him a portable tank of oxygen, borrowed from a Springfield funeral home, to be shared with the other jumpers at high altitudes where the air was thin and cold.

As the twenty parachutists boarded the crowded aircraft, there was disappointment from those who weren't joining them. Twenty-five-year-old Bob Bowsher of Springfield, Ohio, had traveled about 200 miles that morning with his friend Mike Thiem, also of Springfield. Thiem had been one of the "lucky ones" selected to jump. Bowsher lent Thiem his wrist-worn altimeter, since his was a better model than the one Thiem was wearing.

Boarding along with Thiem were Stanley Becka, 25, of Strongsville; Lyle Boyer, 25, Strongsville; James Dreyer, 31, Parma; Richard Patfield, 27, Cleveland; Fred Rivenburg, 25, Springfield; David Sheehan, 30, Medina; Norman Allard, 32, Ashtabula; Jerry Freeman, 32, Akron; Joseph Malarik, 35, Newbury; Dorsie Kitchen, 33, Coventry Township; Ralph Hazelton, 26, Fairview Park; William Onysko, Jr., 27, Canton; Donald Akers, 24, Medina County; James Simmons, 20, Warren.

The two who intended to jump from 30,000 feet were Allan Homestead of Oberlin, a major in the U.S. Air Force who was home on leave, and Larry Hartman of Fairview Park, who had helped plan the jump.

The lone woman selected to make the jump from 20,000 feet was Patricia Lowensbury, 26, of Akron. She and her husband of three years, Alvin, also a skydiver, had driven from their home in Akron that day. Alvin was with his wife at Ortner Airport but was not going to jump, having injured his leg in a jump earlier in the year. He waved as the bomber's motors roared to life and the plane started taxiing down the runway.

It was just after 3 p.m.

That morning at 10 a.m., Allan Homestead had contacted Cleveland Hopkins Airport for a weather forecast and had been told that although substantial cloud cover was expected, there would be enough breaks in the clouds for safe jumping. Homestead had passed the information along to pilot Bob Karns.

Now, at 3 p.m., as the heavily loaded B-25 staggered into the sky over the airport, the cloud cover seemed to have increased, but it was a bright day and there were holes where you could see patches of blue sky.

Ted Murphy, a parachutist who was also a pilot, had come to

Ortner Airport not to take part in the jump but just to watch from the ground. However, after talking with fellow parachutist Louis Pemberton, who had planned to participate in the jump but decided not to after learning of the overcrowding of the B-25, the two decided to fly Murphy's Cessna 180 aircraft to about 12,000 feet over the airfield to take photographs of the jumpers during their descent.

Shortly after the B-25 took off, Murphy's Cessna rolled down the runway, left the ground, and headed for a hole in the clouds. It was flying toward a "perfect storm" of confusion that would lead to tragedy.

It would take Bob Karns nearly an hour to get the heavily loaded B-25 to an altitude of 20,000 feet. At 12,000 feet, he broke through the cloud layer into bright sunlight. Below, all he could see was clouds stretching for miles with just occasional breaks, allowing for a quick glimpse of the Erie County farmland below.

The B-25 was equipped with a VHF radio system that allowed the pilot to talk with the Cleveland Air Route Traffic Control Center, located in Oberlin. The radio also allowed the pilot to home in on the VOR, also called the Omni or Vortac, a navigational aid that sends radio signals in a 360-degree circle, enabling pilots with VHF receivers to determine if they're flying on or to the left or right of a pre-selected course. But the radio in the B-25 could serve both functions at the same time.

Karns's plan had been to fly the old bomber in a circle over the airport until he reached the jump altitude. But because of the clouds thickening below him, he now needed to occasionally check with the air traffic controller for his position on radar. When the plane reached 20,000 feet, Karns would then switch from talking to the radar operator and instead use the VHF receiver to lock on to the VOR and fly directly over the airport to drop the jumpers.

It was a World War II–era B-25 Mitchell bomber, similar to this, from which the eighteen parachutists jumped—unaware they were miles off course and over Lake Erie. *(National Museum of the U.S. Air Force)*

At about this same time, there was a work shift change at the air traffic control center in Oberlin. Controller Engel Smit took over the radar screen that was tracking (among other planes) the B-25 and the Cessna 180, which was now circling high over Ortner Airport. It was later reported, during an investigation, that Smit mistakenly identified the Cessna as the B-25, while the bomber carrying the parachutists was drifting off course ten to twelve miles to the northwest, which carried it out over the lake near Huron, Ohio.

As Karns approached 20,000 feet, he called air traffic control in Oberlin and asked for a heading that would put him on the VOR flying directly over Ortner Airport. Smit, apparently still confusing the Cessna for the B-25, gave Karns the heading for the wrong plane. Karns received the message and, unaware that he was now over Lake Erie, began his run to drop the parachutists.

Karns grabbed the throttles and slowed the plane's speed

from 145 miles per hour to 105. At the same time, he opened the bomb bay doors, causing the aircraft to be filled with sunlight and the roar of the motors and wind. When his calculations indicated that he was over the airport—according to the information he had just received from the air traffic controller—he gave a signal to parachutist Larry Hartman, who was acting as unofficial jumpmaster. Then Hartman, using hand signals and shouts, gave the order to jump. Over the course of thirty seconds, eighteen parachutists leaped through the bomb bay doors and a rear gunner's hatch into the sun-filled sky.

Karns radioed the air traffic control center that the parachute jump had begun.

Bernard "Bud" Johnson, of West Richfield, a former army paratrooper and Green Beret, had been sitting in the aft, or rear, section of the crowded plane when the jump command came. He and others jumped out of a hatch originally installed for use by a gunner in the rear of the aircraft. Johnson was momentarily blinded as he leaped from the darkness of the interior of the aircraft to the brilliant sunlit day above the clouds.

At 20,000 feet, the jumpers were nearly four miles above the earth. Even though it was late summer on the ground, at this altitude the thin air was a bone-chilling -20 to -30 degrees Fahrenheit. Johnson, like most of the jumpers, had worn extra insulated clothing for this jump.

The idea of the high-altitude jump was to do "relative work": In other words, they would free-fall toward earth while practicing maneuvers and even reaching out to touch each other to form skydiving formations before reaching lower altitudes, where they would open their chutes to make a safe landing.

After leaving the B-25, the first fellow-jumper that Bud Johnson saw was Patricia Lowensbury. She was in free-fall just below him. Johnson maneuvered his body closer to hers and reached out his hand. She saw him coming and also reached out, and they briefly slapped hands. They drifted apart and were able to repeat the maneuver again, touching hands before they entered the cloud deck at about 8,000 feet, where Johnson lost sight of her.

Robert Coy of Springfield, Ohio, was sitting in the center of the plane, near the bomb bay doors. When the doors opened and the jump signal was given, he followed fellow parachutists out of the plane and was immediately diving toward earth.

Coy discovered that because of the speed of the plane, the multiple exit points from the B-25, and the wind, the skydivers were scattered, not close together as had been planned for their close-up maneuvering work. He saw a layer of clouds below him and believed the airport was below the clouds.

This was not the first time weather had been instrumental in ruining a jumping experience for Coy. Earlier that summer, he had jumped at 5,500 feet near Tremont City, Ohio, and when he opened his chute, an unexpected wind gust had taken him off-course and carried him over the town. Coy had purposely landed in a large tree to stop his wild ride. He had been able to climb down the tree unhurt.

But this day was different.

Coy said at a press conference that he was "flabbergasted to see water in every direction" as he broke through the cloud layer. He immediately opened his main canopy, hoping it would carry him toward land. It took approximately ninety seconds from the time he opened his chute until his feet touched water. During that brief time, Robert Coy was frantically undoing buckles and straps on his clothing and equipment, trying to prepare for the unexpected water landing.

While all the parachutists on this flight were experienced, and most had had water-landing training, only one of the twenty had a flotation device attached to their equipment—and that one failed to operate.

When they discovered to their surprise that they were going to land in Lake Erie, they had only seconds to prepare.

When Robert Coy hit the water, he estimated he was three to five miles from land. Almost immediately a large wave washed over him, and he swallowed lake water. Still struggling to get out of his boots and heavy equipment, he managed to grab his reserve chute to use as a makeshift float. But the chute soon became waterlogged and sank. He then pulled off his helmet and used it as a float device. But he was rapidly tiring.

"The water was very rough," Coy recalls. "I couldn't see anyone else. All I could hear was the roar of the waves. They were going over my head and swishing down my throat."

Coy was in luck. People on a pleasure boat out for a day of fishing had spotted the parachutes as they headed for the water, and the boat was speeding to help.

Dean Phillips, a Lorain used-car dealer, told the *Elyria Chronicle Telegram* that he had invited his brother-in-law, Richard Ralph, and a friend, Harold Pugh, both of Lorain, to go fishing that day in his 28-foot sport cruiser. He said they were near the Huron Lighthouse off Mitawanga when they first spotted the falling parachutes. They were about one to two miles from where Coy hit the water, and the seas were rough. Phillips had turned the boat around and was traveling as fast as he could safely go with the pounding waves. As they got closer to Coy, they could hear him yelling for help.

As they pulled alongside, Coy shouted, "Thank God, thank God you came!"

After assisting the very grateful Coy into the boat, and as soon as they were sure he was uninjured, the three fishermen resumed the search for downed parachutists.

They saw another canopy still partially inflated a couple of miles away. They struggled through the waves to reach the location and found Bernard "Bud" Johnson of Richfield.

Robert Coy, one of the survivors of the
ill-fated parachute jump into Lake Erie,
is shown here preparing to make a jump
on another day, before the tragedy. *(Courtesy of Robert Coy)*

"I didn't panic," Johnson said later at a press conference. "Not
because of guts, but because I had training. And you don't panic
with training." Johnson said that as he broke through the clouds
and discovered he was over Lake Erie, he suddenly realized he
was going to have to make a water landing. That's when all his
training kicked in. "I knew how to get my suit open real quick
and I opened it. I took everything off and just floated."

Then, Johnson said, something equally unbelievable happened. A pleasure boat approached, and Johnson thought he
was about to be saved. The boat just circled him without offering

to help, and then just as suddenly sped off, leaving the stranded parachutist struggling in the water.

He used his canopy, still partially inflated, for buoyancy to help keep him afloat until other rescuers arrived.

On board Dean Phillips's boat, the rescue effort went on.

They spotted another canopy in the water, but when they pulled it out the harness was empty.

They spotted yet another canopy, and as their boat pulled alongside, they saw that this one had someone under the nylon parachute. They pulled Dorsie Kitchen from the water, still trapped to his parachute and wearing all his equipment. He was not breathing.

Richard Ralph, Phillips's brother-in-law, attempted to resuscitate Kitchen but to no avail. He had been underwater too long. He was dead.

Meanwhile, above the clouds, Robert Karns was still circling in the B-25, thinking he was over the airport and unaware of the tragic mishap and the rescue operation now going on on Lake Erie.

Ted Murphy and Louis Pemberton, also still above in the Cessna, having heard Karns announce that the parachutists had jumped, now realized they could neither see the B-25 nor any of the parachutists doing their high-altitude free-fall, so they decided to return to the airport, land, and try to determine just where the skydivers had jumped.

It was about this time that Karns reached 26,000 feet and radioed air traffic control for permission to climb to 30,000 feet for his second drop. Permission to climb to that altitude was declined because it was getting close to commercial airspace, so Karns asked for a heading that would put him over Ortner Airport. By now the Cessna had landed, and Karns was given a correct heading. When he reached the drop point, the two remaining parachutists, Major Alan Homestead and unofficial jump master Larry Hartman, jumped. Both men did free falls over the cloud deck. Hartman saw the airport through a hole in the clouds and signaled Homestead, and both men aimed for the runway below.

Both landed safely on the airport property.

It was only after Karns landed the B-25 that he and the others waiting on the ground began to learn from radio news reports of the accidental drop of eighteen parachutists into Lake Erie.

Many of them jumped in their cars to drive to Huron to the Town Hall that was serving as center of the search and rescue operation.

Back on Lake Erie, a rescue boat found another parachute with a body still attached. It was Patricia Lowensbury. The mother of three youngsters had apparently become entangled in her equipment when she hit the water and had drowned.

Her husband, Alvin, had driven from Ortner Airport to Huron upon learning of the rescue operation. He was on the dock as they unloaded the body of his wife. In a sad voice he told reporters, "She really loved skydiving."

By early evening, a virtual armada of Coast Guardsmen, police, and volunteers using personal boats were combing miles of Lake Erie near Huron Harbor. Helicopters and airplanes flew low over lake waters that were now becoming increasingly rough, with waves as high as seven feet.

As night fell, the search continued, the lake lit by eerie light from magnesium flares dropped by searching aircraft. Some volunteers lit huge bonfires on beaches near Huron to provide a beacon of light for search parties on the lake.

But by the time dawn broke on Monday, despite the all-night search by hundreds of volunteers, the only parachutists who had been rescued were Bob Coy and Bud Johnson. The only bodies recovered were those of Patricia Lowensbury and Dorsie Kitchen. Fourteen people were still missing.

The search went on.

It would be nearly a week before another body was found. A helicopter flying low about five miles off the mouth of the Huron Harbor spotted it floating in the choppy lake. A Huron police boat was dispatched. They brought the body back to the temporary morgue that had been set up at the Whelan Funeral Home across from the Huron Town Hall.

Bob Bowsher, who had lent his wrist altimeter to Mike Thiem, had been waiting around the Huron Town Hall since the disaster had happened on Sunday. Bowsher was still hoping that somehow his friend had survived, and he was not going home until he knew. He was called to the Whelan Funeral Home to see if he could identify the body the police had brought in from the lake. He could. It was Mike Thiem.

It would be a full week before all the bodies were found and recovered. The last was 20-year-old James Simmons. A fishing boat found his body floating several miles out in the lake.

By the time the search mission ended on September 4, the bodies of sixteen parachutists had been recovered.

It was the worst parachute disaster in history.

Afterward, there were months of investigations. The National Transportation Safety Board in late September 1967 concluded that the pilot of the B-25, Robert Karns, should have terminated the flight because of the heavy cloud cover. They also blamed the air traffic controller at Oberlin, Engel Smit, for apparently misidentifying the Cessna 180 flying over the airport as the B-25, which had drifted out over Lake Erie. (Smit disputed that claim throughout the investigation.) They also blamed the parachutists for jumping into a cloud-filled sky despite the fact that survivors from the jump had said they could not see the ground from the inside of the aircraft and were unaware of the changing cloud conditions.

Robert Coy sent a case of champagne and a thank-you note

to Dean Phillips, Richard Ralph, and Harold Pugh for rescuing him.

Subsequently, the Federal Aviation Administration ordered the suspension of Karns's pilot's license. The agency also fined the only two survivors of the Lake Erie jump—fifty dollars each—for jumping through solid clouds. Robert Coy was almost as flabbergasted by that ruling as he had been when he dropped through the clouds and saw nothing but water below him.

"My attorney at the time advised me to pay the fine, saying it would cost more in time and money to file an appeal," Coy recalls. "I wanted to get the matter over and done with, so I wrote a check."

There was still more tragedy to come.

The B-25, tail number N3443G, was grounded for months as the investigation went on. Eventually it was sold to the Yankee Air Force, Inc., a flying club based in Turner's Falls, Massachusetts. The club planned to use it as a jump plane but never did. The plane was sold again. According to a National Transportation Safety Board report, on August 9, 1970, a ferry pilot, Roger Lopez, was doing a training flight before starting out on the longer journey to the aircraft's new home. Witnesses said he had just completed one touch-and-go landing procedure, had circled, and was coming in for a second touch-down at Orange Municipal Airport, in Orange, Massachusetts, when the B-25 apparently lost power in one engine. It rolled to the left, turned upside down, and crashed onto the runway, where it caught fire and was destroyed. Lopez was killed in the crash.

I was working as a reporter at WJW-TV in Cleveland on August 27, 1967. At about 5 or 6 p.m., the alarm bell on our UPI News teletype machine started ringing, announcing a breaking story. I strolled over to the machine in the corner of the newsroom and glanced down and read: "Several parachutists lost in Lake Erie near Huron, Ohio." Realizing that this was indeed a big story, I called downstairs to our photography department and asked photographer Peter Miller to go with me to Huron. When we arrived, we found dozens and dozens of reporters and cameraman from all over converging on the resort town. We all made our way to the town hall, which had been made into a rescue center for the search-and-recover operations, and there found the two survivors of the jump.

One reporter asked Robert Coy if he would ever jump again from an airplane.

"I don't think so," Coy said. "All of my gear is on the bottom of the lake. I've lost a lot of friends today. This was probably my last jump."

Decades later, Robert Coy recalls what happened after he made that statement. "My mother was a widow, and, although she never complained, I knew that she did not like the fact that I was skydiving. I think that had a lot to do with my decision."

Despite that, just a few days after the Lake Erie accident, Bob borrowed a friend's parachute, drove over to the airfield in Tremont City, and asked his friend "Bud" Neer to take him up in his Cessna.

The two slowly climbed to about 5,000 feet. Bob could see the patchwork of farms and towns below. He nodded to Bud, then stepped out into a clear sky. It was a great jump. At about 2,000 feet he opened his chute. From there, he glided to a perfect landing on the runway of the airport.

That was Bob Coy's last jump.

The Fitchville
Nursing Home Fire

MOST JOURNALISTS DURING their career come across stories so horrific that they wish they could erase the sights and sounds from their memory. One of those stories, for me, occurred early in the morning of November 23, 1963.

It was the morning after President John F. Kennedy was assassinated in Dallas, Texas. Kennedy was the first U.S. president to be assassinated since William McKinley was murdered in office nearly sixty years before.

The nation was reeling. All media attention was focused on Dallas, where the accused assassin, Lee Harvey Oswald, had been captured and was being held at the Dallas Police Department for questioning. Early that morning, Kennedy's body had been flown back to Washington, taken to Bethesda Naval Hospital for an autopsy, and then carried back to the White House to lie in state while his widow, Jacqueline Kennedy, planned his funeral.

I was a reporter at WEOL-AM radio in Lorain at that time. I arrived at the studios, located in the Antlers Hotel, at 4 a.m. to prepare for a sign-on newscast at 5 a.m. and newscasts every half-hour after that until noon.

I had just finished the 5:30 a.m. newscast, an update on the assassination and what was happening in Dallas, when our police and fire scanner came alive with calls for assistance. I was able to figure out from the calls that there was a big fire somewhere in Huron County, near Norwalk, and there were many casualties.

As I gathered more and more information between newscasts, it became clear that this was going to be a major news story.

Fitchville, Ohio, is just a dot on the map. Just north of town, on U.S. Route 250, was the Golden Age Nursing Home. It housed 84 residents, mostly elderly, many with neurological problems.

Pennsylvania truck driver Henry Dahmann, along with his wife, was making a predawn run from Toledo to Cleveland and was passing near Fitchville when he spotted sparks and electrical lines arcing through the pine trees and on the roof of a long L-shaped building. He slammed on his brakes and pulled his truck to the side of the road. Dahmann and his wife ran toward the front door of the building, realizing now that it was a nursing home that was on fire.

Dahmann pounded on the door until a member of the nursing home staff came to investigate the noise and heard Dahmann's urgent shouts that there was fire on the roof. Members of the staff immediately tried to call the fire department, but the telephone line was dead. Dahmann's wife then flagged down another motorist and told them to get to the nearest working telephone and report the fire.

Meanwhile Dahmann and an attendant grabbed fire extinguishers and ran outside to try to extinguish the flaming wires. By the time they exhausted the extinguishers, it appeared that the flames were nearly out. What they did not realize, though, was that the fire was now inside the attic and spreading above the ceiling in the building. When they walked back inside, they found smoke licking down from the ceiling. Now joined by the two other members of the night staff at the nursing home, they

In the early morning hours, fire swept through the Golden Age Nursing Home in Fitchville, Ohio, killing sixty-three residents. It was the worst nursing home fire in American history. *(Cleveland Public Library)*

began trying to get the elderly residents out of the burning building.

Then the lights went out. The fire had burned through the electrical lines to the building. Choking smoke was now complicated by the sudden darkness. People screamed and cried. It was a scene of pure chaos. Some patients who were being led out of the fire turned and ran back into their smoke-filled rooms.

A few of the rescuers had flashlights and were frantically trying to lead the mostly dazed and confused elderly residents out of the building. Those who were able to walk would let the rescuers lead them out of the burning structure, yet once outside, many then tried to go back inside to try to save their possessions.

Twenty-one-year-old seminary student Clifford French and

his 21-year-old wife, Elaine, married just five months, were passing through Norwalk at about 4:30 a.m., headed south on U.S. Route 250. They were traveling from Saginaw, Michigan, to visit Clifford's mother in Wooster, Ohio.

Elaine recalls that she was dozing in the front seat beside her husband while he drove. Besides being a seminary student, he worked a job at General Motors and had ended his workday shortly before they left at midnight to drive to Wooster.

Elaine was suddenly awakened by Clifford yelling, "Look! That building is on fire." She wasn't sure where they were or what the building was as he pulled off the road into a parking lot. Then, they saw the sign on the building: "Golden Age Nursing Home." They could see fire on the roof and people moving around inside the building.

A strong, cold November wind was blowing that morning, and it caused smoke and flames to spread quickly across the attic of the building.

Clifford French jumped out of the car and started toward the front door, telling Elaine to stay outside to help with any people he was able to pull from the burning building. "I remember seeing all them rooms. People all over the place, people in all them rooms," he said, according to the Norwalk *Reflector-Herald*.

Elaine French recalls that he first carried out a small woman. "This little lady was wearing a slip, like you sleep in. It was so cold, and the wind was blowing. I had a coat in the car, so I got it and wrapped her up in that coat."

Elaine saw her husband go back into the burning building again and again to lead or carry elderly residents out.

"As they would bring them out, we would load them into private cars or police cars and they would take them to the hospital," she said.

No ambulances or fire departments had yet reached the site.

When fire and smoke had filled the building, Clifford French made one last trip into the flaming structure. Even fifty years later, Elaine French's voice filled with emotion as she recalled that moment. "He came crawling out on his hands and knees with a woman on his back. The smoke and fire by that time was just terrible and he said, 'I just can't go back in.'" He later told the local newspaper, "If the wind hadn't been blowing we could have gotten them all out. I don't know how long I was in there. It took no time at all for it to be impassable. I couldn't move for the smoke. The last lady I pulled out I was crawling on my hands and knees to get out of there. I'll have to admit, I was mighty scared."

One of the surviving residents, Emmett Evedge, told the Norwalk *Reflector*, "I was awakened by a truck driver and one of the women on the staff of the home. The whole place was full of smoke, people were shouting and crying. You could hear them all over the place."

Evedge told the *Plain Dealer* that he and another fellow pushed as many as they could out the door before the heat and smoke drove them out of the building.

Finally, nearly twenty-five minutes after truck driver Henry Dahmann and his wife first spotted the fire, the first fire department arrived. The New London Fire Department, located about seven miles away, pulled up to find the entire Golden Age Nursing Home, a 186-by-65-foot structure, engulfed in flames. Fire was leaping from windows and doors. The tar on the roof was boiling and splashing onto the ground.

"There was no way to get into that building," Chief Al Walter of the New London Fire Department told me in an interview at the time. "There was nothing we could do but put water on it."

The Greenwich Village Fire Department arrived next.

"There just wasn't anything we could do," Fire Chief Dave Seidel recalls. "It was totally out of control."

This is the sight that greeted firefighters when they finally were able to enter the building: row upon row of burned beds, many of them containing human remains. *(Courtesy of Tri-Community Fire Department)*

Firefighters quickly learned the scope of the tragedy. The nursing home staff told them they had 84 residents in the home, and fewer than two dozen had been rescued. And some of those had been badly injured in the fire.

The fire was roaring. Anything in the building that could burn was burning. Other fire departments from surrounding communities arrived, but all they could do was continue to pour water on the raging inferno. The roof collapsed. Walls crumbled from the intense heat. Black, angry smoke rolled into the morning sky.

Rescuers next faced a crucial problem: a lack of water. No water mains ran to this remote location. Responding firefighters had to truck in the water they needed, and with a fire burning out of control they would need a lot of it. Some tanker trucks

Funeral home attendants and firefighters had the grisly job of locating and carrying out the charred bodies from the burned-out nursing home. *(Courtesy of Tri-Community Fire Department)*

were able to refill at nearby farm ponds, but others had to go as far as New London to refill.

Firefighters from New London, North Fairfield, and Greenwich (Fitchville did not have a fire department) fought the flames throughout the morning until there was nothing left but piles of smoldering rubble and a few walls that indicated where the nursing home had once stood.

At about 10:30 a.m., firefighters were first able to enter what was left of the building and start digging through the rubble. They knew what they were going to find: scenes that would haunt them for years to come.

"It looked like piles of burned newspapers," Elaine French says, remembering the rows and rows of blackened beds and the bodies.

In one doorway was a fire-blackened wheelchair jammed in a not-wide-enough doorframe. In the chair were the charred remains of what had once been a human being. Behind the door were bodies of several other residents who had been trapped behind the wheelchair when it could not get through the door.

Elaine French said she could see among the remains of the building a wheelchair jammed into a closet door frame where one resident, in an attempt to escape the flames, lost his life trying to hide in the closet. She choked up as she recalled the scene. "I remember the smell. Burning flesh," she says.

Other bodies were found underneath beds, most burned beyond recognition.

Firefighters who were there that day later recalled it for a documentary: "It was unreal," one said. "Everything was burned, but the beds were still lined up in a row and some of the victims were still in their beds." Another said he saw "the remains of a person. They had some kind of restraints on them, holding them." (The documentary, *Fireland*, by Justin Zimmerman, can be found on YouTube.)

It was nearly noon when I arrived in Fitchville. Using my media credentials, I was able to get past police barricades. I learned that the Ohio State Highway Patrol had taken over the gymnasium at the Fitchville Elementary School to be used as a temporary morgue when bodies were finally recovered.

Huron County coroner Dr. William Holman, then in his first year on the job, had been called to the scene to oversee the grim task of locating each of the victims and identifying them.

That was going to be a very difficult job because files, papers, and even personal possessions of the victims had all been destroyed by the flames. The victims were even in worse shape. Most bodies had arms and legs burned off, and some even had skulls burned away. All that remained were torsos. Firefighters were cautioned by Dr. Holman to use only a light spray of water

The main entrance was about all that remained after the fire. It is believed that the blaze started in the roof above this doorway. *(Cleveland Public Library)*

on the still smoldering beds so that what was left of the bodies was not further destroyed.

A fire chief who was overseeing the grisly job told me the firefighters and funeral home workers did "yeoman's work" that morning.

I silently watched as firefighters methodically went through the ruins, using their hands to dig into the still-smoking rubble by each bed looking for human remains.

Authorities, working with the nursing home staff, had drawn up a map of the interior showing where each bed was located and which patient was assigned to that bed. When firemen found human remains in or near a bed, a representative of a local funeral home would bring a body bag and then carry the remains into the parking lot, where a number would be placed on the bag corresponding to the bed where it was found.

Some bodies were identified by other means. Dr. Holman later recalled for the documentary *Fireland*, "There was one man who had red hair, and we found him out in the corridor. Some of the concrete block had fallen across his upper trunk and head, and when we uncovered the rest of him, there was his red hair. So that's how we identified him."

Another body was identified by the fact that he had an artificial leg. The leg survived the fire and was found next to the badly charred body.

"It was my job to identify them," Dr. Holman said. "Under the circumstances we did the best we could, but we couldn't be 100 percent positive."

In the 1960s, ambulance service in rural areas was usually provided by local funeral directors. On the morning of November 23rd, there were also dozens of ambulances and their crews from surrounding communities at the fire scene.

As the noon hour passed, an Ohio State Highway Patrol car drove through the barricades. It was carrying Ohio governor James A. Rhodes. Rhodes had been planning to fly to Washington, D.C., to pay his respects to the fallen president.

Firefighters were still hosing down hotspots in the rubble as I watched them and county officials brief the governor. He seemed visibly shaken as he viewed the rows of twisted, burned, metal beds still smoking. When the breeze shifted, you could still detect the unmistakable smell of burning human flesh.

The governor ordered state fire marshal Fred Rice to personally head up "an intensive" investigation as to what had caused the fire, then left to continue his trip to Washington.

"There was plenty of time to get everyone out, but the elderly patients just didn't seem to understand what was going on," Mrs. Tenny Wireman told the *Mansfield News Journal*. Wireman, a

This aerial photo by photographer Tom Root shows just how total the destruction was of the Golden Age Nursing Home. *(Courtesy of the Tom Root family and the New London Area Historical Society Museum)*

cleaning woman at the nursing home who had helped rescue some of the residents, continued, "When we went to tell the patients there was a fire, they just sat down. They never seemed to know what was going on . . . Many of the patients in one ward were real bad mental patients and could not comprehend their own danger."

According to a *Sandusky Register* article, Sandusky truck driver John J. Minier, who also stopped to help, told fire authorities that "Fire started above the electric light box outside the building. At first there wasn't too much smoke or flame but within fifteen minutes the place was filled with smoke. We had to stop helping them then."

By late afternoon, firefighters had recovered sixty-two bodies

Police and funeral home aides took over the Fitchville Elementary School to serve as a temporary morgue. Body bags containing the charred remains of the fire victims were brought here for identification and to be claimed by their next of kin. *(Cleveland Public Library)*

in the burned-out building. (A sixty-third, and final, body would be found the next day.) The dead, as they were identified, were loaded into an ambulance and taken to the temporary morgue at the school, where families of the victims could come and claim the remains.

The families arrived during the next few days, and some had questions. Mrs. Ethel Schwenk of East Cleveland told the *Plain Dealer* that the first notice she had that her 71-year-old father, Samuel B. Rood, was a resident of the Golden Age Nursing Home was when she learned of his death.

"I thought he was at Prospect Nursing Home here (in E. Cleveland). I didn't know he'd been transferred to Fitchville Home until I read a list of victims." The Prospect Nursing

Home blamed the lack of notification on state officials who had approved the transfer.

There were other, similar stories.

At that time, it was not uncommon practice to transfer nursing home residents who were under state care from one facility to another without giving notice to the families.

The owner of the Golden Age Nursing Home, Robert W. Pollack, blamed the majority of deaths on panic. "Instead of going out the doors, they went back to their beds," he told the *Plain Dealer.*

The building had been inspected by state officials in March 1963, and no violations had been reported.

In the days to come, there would be several investigations into the fire.

A Huron County grand jury took a look at the events of November 23rd and came to the conclusion that no indictment would be issued. They determined that the fire was caused by an electrical short circuit. Their report did say that existing state fire inspections were valueless and urged state legislators to change the regulations for nursing homes.

State fire marshal Fred Rice, as ordered by the governor, spent five weeks interviewing police, firefighters, and survivors of the blaze. On December 31 he issued a report with three main points: First, the probable cause of the fire was extensive shorting along over-fused and improperly wired electrical circuits. Second, the probable cause of the extensive fire damage was the nearly simultaneous ignition of fires at a number of different points as well as a delay in turning in the alarm to the fire department. Third, the extensive loss of life was a result of a lack of prompt evacuation based on an orderly plan. He summed up the report by saying the fire was caused not by design but by carelessness.

All this meant little to those who had lost loved ones in the

Twenty-one bodies, victims of the fire, were unclaimed. Huron County funeral directors combined their resources and arranged a mass funeral for them on Friday, November 29, 1963, at Woodlawn Cemetery in Norwalk, Ohio. *(Cleveland Public Library)*

fire. By the following week, hearses from funeral homes from all over northern Ohio had come and carried away, one-by-one, bodies that families had claimed. Now officials faced a new problem. About two-thirds of the bodies were removed by relatives, but a large number of the dead still, for one reason or another, had not been claimed by family members.

In some cases, the family just could not afford the cost of a funeral. In other cases, the resident had no relatives listed.

When it became clear that a total of twenty-one of the fire victims' bodies were not going to be claimed, the funeral directors in Huron County came together and offered to provide final services for these last fire fatalities.

On Friday, November 29, 1963, I was standing near a small

Two heroes of the fire, Elaine and
Clifford French, on their wedding
day. Six months later they would
both help rescue many people from
the burning nursing home. *(Courtesy
of Elaine French)*

crowd of mourners at Woodlawn Cemetery in Norwalk, Ohio.
I still remember the sight of one black funeral hearse after
another driving slowly into the cemetery. There were twenty-one hearses, one for each person whose body had gone
unclaimed. Each of the twenty-one identical caskets had a large
flower display. They were buried in a sixty-foot-long grave.

Later, a memorial stone containing each of the twenty-one
names was placed nearby.

The entire cost was paid for by funeral directors in Huron
County.

The event was largely ignored by national media because of
the focus on the Kennedy assassination.

In the years to come, laws would be passed requiring nursing homes to have sprinkler systems, interior fire alarms, fire drills, and evacuation plans. Many of these laws were based on what happened in rural Huron County on November 23, 1963.

People who were there that morning will never forget it.

"For months after that we both had nightmares and I would wake up screaming," Elaine French recalled. "I could still see the flames." Her husband, the Reverend Clifford French, who rescued several people from the fire, passed away in 2011 at the age of 69.

As of this writing, more than fifty years have passed, and the Fitchville nursing home fire still is considered to be one of the worst nursing home fires in American history.

The Xenia Tornado

APRIL 3, 1974, was a warm spring day in Central Ohio.

A formation of Canada geese flew noisily over the recently built Ohio State Highway Patrol Post 29 on State Route 68, south of the town of Xenia.

Sergeant Jim Debevec, the acting post commander, and Trooper Gary Taylor were at the rear of the post by their patrol cars when the geese overhead caught their attention. Jim Debevec isn't sure why, but he always thinks of those geese when he recalls what happened that day.

As the geese flew away, the two men's attention was drawn to a huge black cloud that stretched from the heavens to the earth.

"Look at that," Debevec said. "What in the world is that?"

What they were seeing was hell on earth: an F5 tornado, the most vicious and strongest whirlwind that occurs on the planet.

And it was heading straight for Xenia.

It was part of a storm system that would come to be known as a "super outbreak" of tornadoes—the most violent tornado outbreak ever recorded, as thirty F4 and F5 tornadoes spawned throughout the Midwest. The worst of those would hit the town of Xenia, Ohio, at about 4:30 that afternoon.

Trooper Gary Taylor recalls that the storm appeared to be headed for the Stadium Heights neighborhood, where his home was. His wife Roberta (Bobbie) and their two daughters, Jolene, age 6, and Angelene, age 2, would be home at this hour.

Gary Taylor had to get to them. He leaped into his patrol car, drove rapidly out of the patrol driveway, and headed toward the oncoming storm.

Meanwhile, at the Taylor home, Bobbie Taylor and her two girls were in a second-floor family room. Bobbie said she was running the vacuum cleaner while the girls were watching a children's show on WHIO-TV. Suddenly, her older daughter, Jolene, got her attention and pointed to the TV screen. The broadcast had been interrupted, and the station was issuing a tornado warning. Bobbie ran to a window and looked out. Seeing an immense black whirling cloud, she immediately grabbed the youngsters and rushed down the stairs, through the kitchen, and down another flight of stairs into the basement, where they huddled in the southwest corner. Bobbie was lying on top of her daughters as the storm hit their house.

Gary Taylor was trying to run parallel to the storm in his state patrol car. He got so close to the tornado at one point that the front of his car was jumping up and down because of the wind. He turned away and tried another route, driving through downtown Xenia, which had just been hit by the storm. Trees and electrical lines were down. Roads were filled with debris. He took to the back streets.

At the intersection of Monroe and Main Street he was maneuvering around downed power lines when something caught his eye: A man was being robbed—in the middle of a deadly storm. The unconscious victim was lying in the street as another man went through his pockets. Taylor slammed on his brakes and jumped out of the car, yelling at the thief. The looter looked up, saw the police officer, and immediately ran away. Taylor rushed to the injured man, who had apparently been hit by flying debris. He was bleeding profusely and was unconscious. Taylor went to his car and radioed for an ambulance, then grabbed his first aid kit and went back to put a pressure bandage on the man to halt

This frightening photo of the approaching tornado was taken from the Greene Memorial Hospital looking southeast from Wilson Drive, where the tornado was tearing through Meadow Lane and Louise Drive. The hospital escaped damage. *(National Weather Service, courtesy of the Greene County Historical Society)*

the bleeding. He waited until the ambulance arrived. As soon as the injured man was taken care of, Taylor got back in his car and continued his journey home to make sure his family was safe.

In the basement of their home, Bobbie Taylor and her daughters could hear glass breaking along with the roar of the wind. "The storm was so loud," she recalls. "It was louder than a freight train." The house above them was creaking. The lights went out. Things were falling. "It was like it went on forever," Bobbie said, "but it really was over in just a few minutes, and then we were trapped in our basement."

The wind had moved the house off its foundation and collapsed the roof onto the front porch. The house was in shambles. Glass was gone from all the windows. The door to the basement was jammed shut.

A neighbor's son heard Bobbie's screams for help and was able to unblock the door, releasing the mother and two daughters.

Finally, Gary Taylor had reached the Stadium Heights neighborhood, but the damage was so severe that he could not get to his street. He left his patrol car and ran across several back yards until he saw what was left of his home. Bobbie and his two daughters were in the front yard waiting for him. He was relieved to find that, other than a few scratches, his wife and daughters were safe.

There was even more damage—and loss of life—in the Arrowhead subdivision on the edge of town. Many of the houses there did not have basements.

Cathy Wilson lived in one of those houses. She was nine years old.

"My four-year-old sister, Elaine, and I were outside playing when we saw the big black, boiling cloud," she recalls now. "I told my mother, Lois, and she told us to go get in the closet." There was no room in the closet, so her mother next told the children to get in the empty bathtub. "So we got into the bathtub, and I got on top of my sister and my mother got on top of both of us."

She remembered the sounds.

"All the doors slammed shut because of the pressure. All the windows broke out. And we could hear the glass swirling and hitting the house. The sound was more like a jet engine. It was this horrible sound. Someone recorded it, and I can't listen to it. It gives me creeps. It seemed like it lasted a very long time. We looked up at the bathroom ceiling and we could see blue skies. And in the hole was a purple washcloth. We didn't own a purple washcloth."

Houses on both sides of the Wilson home were gone.

Vicki Payer also lived in the Arrowhead subdivision. It was

The storm passed through the heart of downtown Xenia. This view is southwest of the courthouse, where cars were flipped, trees were downed, and businesses were heavily damaged. *(Courtesy of the Greene County Historical Society)*

her son Jon's 4th birthday. They were planning a small family party that evening, just Jon and his sisters, Teri Lynn, age 5, and Traci, almost 3. The kids wanted to play outside, but rain was starting to sprinkle down so Vicki told them to stay inside. When she heard the roar of the oncoming storm, she told the kids to go into the bathroom because they had no basement.

She then started to head for the bedroom to wake her husband, Terry, an Ohio state highway patrolman, who, after working the night shift, was still sleeping. He came out of the bedroom about the same time and said, "Let's go," and herded the entire family into their bathroom just as the storm hit.

"The back wall of the bathroom came down on me," Vicki recalls. "We were sheltering the kids between us. The wind picked up our son, Jon, and Terry had to pull him back down." Had it not been for Terry's quick action, his son might have been sucked out of the bathroom and become another of the Arrowhead casualties.

In minutes it was over. The Payer family had to dig out from under a wall that had collapsed on them and crawl out of the wreckage that had once been their home. They had all survived.

One of the first things they saw was that their neighbor's house was completely gone. Only a water heater still stood. Another neighbor, Ken Steele, coming to check on the Payer family, found a man rifling through the trunk of Terry Payer's demolished patrol car, which had been parked in the driveway with their two other cars that were also destroyed in the storm. The looter was attempting to steal a shotgun that was stored there. Steele confronted the man, who dropped the shotgun and ran off.

The *Columbus Dispatch* reported that William Jones of Arrowhead was in downtown Xenia trying to get home when "his house collapsed on top of his wife, Mary's, head. 'She was in the bathroom between the tub and the water closet,' Jones said, pointing to rubble where his wife was trapped. 'When I got here she was out in the yard, barefoot, screaming and running around.' She was taken to a Dayton hospital with a concussion and shock."

Chief Deputy Morgan, of the Greene County Sheriff's Office, was quoted in the *Columbus Dispatch* saying "the tornado cut a swath through the city six to eight blocks wide. Destruction in the path of the twister was near total. Many homes were carried on top of others. One rescuer said a woman came up to him and asked, 'Where's my baby?' He said he didn't know what to tell them."

The winds demolished the front of a local supermarket, yet sixty-five customers inside were not injured. In a bar next door, though, two people were killed.

The *Xenia Daily Gazette* (whose building suffered heavy

The force of the tornadic winds was so strong that it picked up a
semi-tractor trailer and deposited it on top of a local bowling alley.
(Courtesy of the Greene County Historical Society)

damage in the storm) reported five persons dead at the A&W
Root Beer stand on Dayton Avenue, including an entire family:
Paul Wisscup, age 25, his wife Sue Ann, 19, and their daughter
Amy, just 18 months old, were killed when the storm hit the
restaurant. Bodies from several locations were gathered at the
root beer stand for transportation to other facilities.

Gene Fischer, the current sheriff of Greene County, related
this story, told to him when he was a Xenia police officer by
Donald Hubbard, his training officer. Hubbard, a patrol officer
at the time of the tornado, had been assigned to use the public
address system on his police car and drive through the streets
of downtown Xenia warning people to take cover. However, the
tornado caught up with Hubbard. He suddenly lost control of
the car, which the wind started to spin like a top. Hubbard was

able to crawl under his dashboard as the car kept spinning. The tornado finally released the car, and Hubbard, unbelievably, was not injured.

Daniel Hon, a state patrol officer, was also in downtown Xenia when the tornado hit. He was off duty and didn't have to go to work until late that evening, so he decided to get a haircut at the Central Barber Shop across from the Greene County Courthouse. The shop was run by a man named Charlie. A customer was already in the barber chair, so Hon offered to go next door to a cafe and get coffee for the three of them. He was just returning to the barber shop when he looked up at the sky.

"When I came out the door I looked west, towards Dayton, and I saw the tops of buildings going down the street [flying through the air]," he recalls.

He ran back into the barber shop to warn Charlie and his customer, and the three of them ran out onto the sidewalk, where two steel doors led to a basement.

"There was a lady there staring down the street," he says. "We grabbed her and took her with us into the basement. The air pressure was so strong by that time we could not close the doors. We were at the bottom of the stairs, peeking around the corner watching debris and cars blow down the street."

The storm passed in just a few minutes, but when they came out of the cellar Hon recalled what they saw. "The town was pretty much a mess. Charlie's shop was pretty much destroyed. Charlie's comment was, 'Fellows, I'm closed.'"

Hon rushed to his car and found it covered in debris, its windshield broken. So he started to run home. But after about a block he suddenly realized that his house was several miles away. He ran back to his car, cleared it of debris, and drove off, peering through the smashed windshield. Fortunately, his family was safe, and his house had sustained minimal damage.

The *Xenia Daily Gazette* reported that parents roamed the

streets in the Arrowhead subdivision looking for children and spouses. Husbands tried to find their homes and families, some without luck. Nine people in this subdivision would die, many of them children.

I was working at WJW-TV in Cleveland at the time. I was just ending my shift when I was asked to take a camera crew and go to Medina to cover storm damage there. Photographer Peter Miller, sound engineer Gary Korb, and I had just reached Medina when we received a call on our two-way radio canceling that assignment and telling us to head instantly to Xenia, where a much larger and more deadly storm had hit.

It took us almost three hours, driving as fast as we could through, at times, torrential rains. It was about 9 p.m. when we got to Xenia. All major roads into the city were blocked. Authorities were letting no one into the area. Peter Miller had an idea. We were in a black four-door sedan with antennas on the trunk lid. Miller had a press badge issued several years before by the Cuyahoga County Sheriff's Department. He tried another street into town. This time, as we approached the barricade, he held the badge out the window, and they waved us through the checkpoint.

All three of us were veteran journalists and had seen tornado damage before, but this was different. It reminded us of scenes of bombed-out cities after World War II. Rescuers in the growing darkness were going through the wreckage of homes and businesses searching for victims and survivors.

One of the first things that caught my eye was the shredded treetops. Pieces of roofing and articles of clothing were wrapped around tree limbs as if the town were preparing for some macabre holiday.

A Penn Central freight train had been blown over by the winds, right in the center of town. The locomotives were still on the tracks, but the freight cars had spilled into the parking lots

Aftermath of the F-5 tornado that hit Xenia, part of a "super outbreak."
The base of the storm was more than a half-mile wide. *(United States Air
Force, Wright-Patterson AFB)*

of a nearby Kroger and a used car business. The grocery store
was destroyed.

One odd scene I recall was on North Allison Avenue: A row
of bar stools stood out in the open. The Mr. Donut shop that
once housed them was completely gone. The stools were all that
remained.

The tornado had ripped its way along Detroit Street, one of
Xenia's main streets, for about a mile. The winds had collapsed
dozens of homes, knocked down walls, and left so much debris
that it took bulldozers several hours to clear a lane down the
street.

A disaster center was set up in the county jail where the Red
Cross worked to reunite families.

The Arrowhead subdivision was one of the worst hit residential areas in the Xenia tornado. Many of the homes were flattened or heavily damaged. *(United States Air Force, Wright-Patterson AFB)*

Darkness was adding to the chaos. The electricity was out. There was no phone service. And residents were being warned to boil water before using it.

By midnight about 100 survivors of the storm had come to the YMCA, which was serving as a shelter. A clerk, 20-year-old Linda Frank, served food and offered cots and blankets. Many people were still in shock and appeared frightened.

At the Kroehler Manufacturing Company, a tractor trailer rig had been blown about 100 yards onto the roof of the Community Lanes Bowling Alley across the street.

North from the center of town, the James SuperValu Store on East Market Street was destroyed, and almost all of the older homes on North Detroit Street were in ruins. Little was left of Xenia High School, where the wind had heaved school buses into the building. Police reported that six schools were destroyed.

Ohio state patrol officer Kenneth "KO" Martin had just come off duty on April 3rd and arrived at his home on the southeast side of Xenia on Murray Hill Drive to see the tornado warning issued on local TV. He herded his wife, Sandra, and children Rebel, age 5, Kelli, 4, and Kenni, 1, down the street to a neighbor's house that had a basement. Then he and a couple of neighbors went into the back yard and watched as three separate tornadoes approached the town and seemed to meld into one giant twister.

Martin's house escaped with only minor damage. Martin then put his uniform back on and drove to the patrol post south of town to see what he could do to help.

As the evening went on and the body count began to climb, the small morgue at the Greene County Hospital ran out of room. Martin was given the grim assignment of going to the Ohio Soldiers and Sailors Orphan Home and turning its gymnasium into a temporary morgue.

"We put tarps over the gym floor and turned the air conditioning as low as it would go and started laying out the bodies in rows on the gym floor," Martin later recalled. It was his job to try to identify each body as best he could. He would write details on a tag—"male, age approximately 20 years old, brown hair, approximate weight . . . "—and then attach that tag to the body bag containing that person. The hardest part of that evening was when they brought in a child. "It made a tough job even tougher," he said.

It was a couple of days before officials finally determined that thirty-three people had died in the storm. Over a thousand people had been injured. During the cleanup, two National Guardsmen on duty to prevent looting were killed when the

Ohio State Highway patrol officer Gary
Taylor was frantically trying to reach his
family during the tornado when he broke
up a robbery in progress and stopped to
aid an unconscious man. Taylor lost his
home in the tornado. Fortunately, his
family survived. *(Courtesy of Gary and Bobbie
Taylor)*

damaged furniture store they were sheltered in caught fire.
Their deaths brought the final total to thirty-five killed as a
result of the tornado.

My camera crew and I wrapped up our coverage of the
tornado about noon the following day. We had been working for
more than thirty hours, and we had a three-hour drive ahead
of us back to Cleveland. We were tired, dirty, and hungry. I did
my final report in front of the Greene County Courthouse. The
lawn was scattered with gargoyles that had been ripped from
the courthouse roof by the storm. A huge tree nearby had been
uprooted. But in front of me as I did my final TV wrap up was

a statue commemorating the Ten Commandments—it had not been touched by the tornado.

Days after the storm, The *Columbus Dispatch* reported that a resident in Mt. Gilead, Ohio, found in his front yard a catalogue addressed to a home in Xenia, almost ninety miles away.

Through the generosity of a Xenia businessman, a new apartment complex was made available to police and firemen whose homes had been destroyed in the storm. Gary and Bobbie Taylor moved in there, as did Terry and Vicki Payer. Cathy Wilson and her family were able to move in with a relative in nearby Beavercreek, Ohio. Today Cathy Wilson is the executive director of the Greene County Historical Society, and she has on display there the purple washcloth that floated into their bathroom during the tornado.

Dan Hon, who took shelter and watched the storm from a barber shop basement, probably reflects the feelings of all the survivors I spoke to in the writing of this story.

"The people who survived just don't forget," he told me. "Each year at 4:40 p.m. on April the 3rd, I make a toast to the memory of the people who didn't survive."

The Blizzard of '78

I WAS AWAKENED on Thursday, January 26, 1978, by the roar of the wind and the creaking sound of the roof of the two-story apartment building in which I lived in Rocky River, Ohio.

Dawn was breaking as I made my way to a window and looked outside into a world of pure white. It was the start of a two-day blizzard, later called "The White Hurricane," that brought Ohio, along with much of the Midwest, to its knees.

Two major weather systems in the upper atmosphere had collided, triggering what weather forecasters would later term a megastorm. Whatever you want to call it, it was quite simply the worst winter storm to hit Ohio in the twentieth century.

Severe blizzard conditions were sweeping across the state: high winds, blowing and drifting snow, and temperatures plunging into the single digits and below. Conditions became steadily worse as the hours went by.

The first area of Ohio to be hit was the Cincinnati area, about 1 a.m., as 60-mile-per-hour winds drove the falling snow into road-clogging drifts. In nearby Warren County, the Mason-Montgomery Road had been plowed so many times already that night that the buildup on the sides of the road coupled with drifting snow created a tunnel-like effect for drivers.

John London, a reporter on WLW radio in Cincinnati, was

at home. Seeing the white-out conditions, he called the station and asked if he should come in to work. News director Bill Ridenour said that many staffers had already called in to say it was impossible to get to the station, which was located at that time at 4th and Vine in Cincinnati. London, too, said it was impossible to drive on the snow-clogged streets, but he told the news director he would walk to work.

"The news director tried to talk me out of it because of the danger," he recalls. "I was young, 27 or 28 years old, and had always been a walker and runner." So he put on all the clothes he could think of—several tee shirts, a sweatshirt, a hooded sweatshirt, plus a wool beanie-style hat, jeans with sweatpants over them, boots, and a double pair of gloves—and set out walking from his home on Harrison in Westwood.

"The landscape was surreal," London said. "Everywhere you looked. And bitter, bitter, cold. It sounds overly dramatic, but it was like being on another planet." There was snow and ice everywhere. "You could see every breath you took."

London struggled through seven miles of snow-filled streets and sidewalks facing wind gusts of up to 50 miles per hour.

"I don't remember seeing a single person or car that morning. At first it was kind of exciting, but as time went on I began to think maybe this wasn't a very good idea. It was like the world was just frozen in place." London is not sure how long it took him to reach WLW. "When I finally reached the studios, I had to thaw out quite a while before I was able to go on the air."

London found the town at a standstill. Mayor Gerald "Jerry" Springer was urging nonessential businesses to close during the storm and motorists to stay off the roads. The U.S. Postal Service had announced they were suspending carrier mail service that day for the safety of the letter carriers. The Ohio River had frozen and was clogged by large blocks of ice. "That was unusual," London said. "I had some friends that walked across the frozen river. I didn't try it. It was like the arctic had set up shop here in Ohio."

By 3 a.m., the storm had moved north through Dayton and then Columbus, the howling winds bringing down electric and telephone lines. Blowing snow stopped movement on the highways.

By 7 a.m., the huge storm roared into Cleveland.

Now, it blanketed almost the entire state.

I was a reporter at WJW-TV in Cleveland. The station was located on the lakefront about fourteen miles from my home, so I decided I had better start for work. The drive usually took me about twenty minutes. This morning it took nearly three hours!

Stalled cars were everywhere. Traffic, when it moved, only crawled along. When cars stopped, drifting snow would gather around the wheels. When the opportunity to move came, you could hear the wheels just spin.

I watched as debris from an apartment roof fell into the snow-covered street. A corrugated steel bus shelter suddenly blew in front of my car. Mostly, though, it was hard to see much at all because of the constant whiteouts caused by the increasing winds.

A radio report told of a lake freighter frozen in the ice off Sandusky that had just recorded a wind gust of 110 miles per hour and sustained winds of 80 miles per hour.

I was unwilling to brave the lakefront Shoreway and so made my way slipping and sliding on side streets through downtown Cleveland. Approaching East Ninth Street, I could see flashing lights. Police had shut off parts of the street because high winds were causing glass windows to blow out of the tall buildings, and bits of glass were raining down on streets and sidewalks.

By now I had been driving more than two hours and had gone about ten miles. When I finally reached the intersection of East Fifty-fifth Street and South Marginal Road, where the television station was located, I found the road almost blocked by drifting snow. Fortunately, a private snowplowing firm had opened a single lane to the driveway of the station.

The storm now seemed to be coming from all directions, and wind was whistling full force across the surface of Lake Erie, driving the snow across the Shoreway and South Marginal Road as I slipped and slid the short distance to the TV8 driveway. When I attempted to turn, I slid forward into a snowbank, nearly burying the front of my car. All attempts to back up failed, so I shut off the motor and prepared to abandon my car and walk the rest of the way to the station door.

Before leaving home that morning, I had dressed in just about every piece of cold-weather gear I had: my old Marine Corps "Mickey Mouse" thermal boots, long underwear, heavy wool pants, a wool shirt, sweater, and a surplus air force arctic parka, along with scarf and gloves. I probably resembled the Michelin Man as I struggled against the blinding snow up to the station door. I was coated from head to toe in snow and ice by the time I stumbled into the lobby.

Virgil Dominic, TV8's news director at the time, remembers that day. "The broadcasting schedule was thrown out the window. We started our newscasts on time and then just kept on going. There was so much going on. So much updating that needed to be done. Dick Goddard and our other meteorologists were on the air every few minutes giving out the latest information and trying to keep people safe."

Cleveland's mayor in 1978 was Dennis Kucinich. He and his then-wife, Sandra, had flown to Washington, D.C., the day before for a meeting with President Jimmy Carter. With news of the terrible storm that was hitting Ohio, Mayor Kucinich was frantically trying to get back to Cleveland. Flights all over the Midwest were being cancelled because of the high winds and blinding snow. Against the wishes of his wife, he was now

In northwestern Ohio, the blizzard nearly buried some buildings. It would be days or weeks before they could dig out. *(Courtesy of the Ohio State Highway Patrol)*

attempting to charter a small business jet that could get him to any airport in Ohio; from there, he vowed, he would find any kind of transportation, even a snowmobile, to get him back to Cleveland City Hall.

In the meantime, by telephone, Kucinich instructed finance director Joseph Tegreene—now serving as the acting mayor in Kucinich's absence—to take command of the city's battle against the street-clogging snow. At age 24, Tegreene found himself in charge of Ohio's largest city.

"You wanted to do something," Tegreene recalls, "but you just couldn't. I was awakened in the pre-dawn hours and told a police car was being sent to take me to City Hall. I said, 'Why?' Then I looked outside and understood. Nothing was moving. Cars were abandoned in the middle of the street.

"When we got to City Hall, I tried to call department heads, and many of them also could not get to work. I found myself talking with a snow truck operator who told me, quite truthfully, that everything that could be done was being done, but as quickly as they would plow, say, the Shoreway, the winds would cover it right over, and it would look like they had never been there.

"We called the radio and television stations and pleaded with people to stay home and off the streets. I ordered the recreation centers opened as shelters for those that had no heat or electricity."

Tegreene talked with the governor's office and the Ohio National Guard but got the feeling that, while they were sympathetic to the problems, the crippling storm was statewide and was overwhelming everyone.

According to a *Sandusky Register* article, one of the first deaths in the storm was 48-year-old Veronica Wright, a nurse's aide from Huron, Ohio. She was attempting to go to work that morning when her car became stuck in a drift. She apparently left the car to find help, and even though there were houses nearby, the wind and snow disoriented her, and she wandered off the road into a field. She was found there the next day, frozen to death.

Erie County became the first county in the state to call for the National Guard. An hour before Governor James Rhodes declared an emergency, Erie County sheriff Harold Gladwell issued a call for guardsmen. Gladwell said conditions were so bad in Erie County that he could not wait for the governor to act. With power lines down throughout the county and many roads impassable due to snow, Gladwell told the *Plain Dealer*, "The only thing in operation now are some snowmobiles and tractors, we are completely blizzarded in."

Major General John Clem, adjutant general of the Ohio National Guard, told the *Plain Dealer* that more than two thousand guard troops were called to duty and were mainly patrolling highways, checking snowbound cars for anyone trapped inside. "We're at a real disadvantage," Clem said. "We can't use helicopters because of the wind and snow, and on the ground, at best, we can't see fifteen feet ahead of us." He said his men had rescued many stranded truckers along interstate highways near Columbus and Dayton.

In Central Ohio, the *Marion Star* reported that, due to strong winds, drifting snow had completely buried some one-story homes.

At that time, Mary Ellen Withrow was the county treasurer in Marion County. She recalls being snowed in on her family farm. Drifts covered the roads, and she and her husband Norman, a rural mail carrier, and their 13-year-old daughter, Rebecca, had awakened to find themselves snowbound. What most concerned Withrow was the fact that she had sent the county's tax bills to the post office the day before with instructions to deliver them on January 26th. With the ferocity of the storm, she worried that many of the bills might get lost. But there was nothing she could do. She discovered her electric service and her phone had also gone out because of the high winds and snow.

"The only heat we had in the house was a wood-burning fireplace," Withrow recalls. "We huddled around that for days." Her husband would go out in the storm to gather wood, which he would pile in their basement so it would be dry enough to burn. "We had raised sweet potatoes that year, so we had plenty in the basement, and we cooked them over the fireplace. We ate a lot of sweet potatoes in that storm."

I had just walked into the WJW-TV newsroom when I was assigned to check out a report that Cleveland police were trying to reach several cars that had become snowbound on Brookpark Road near Cleveland Hopkins Airport.

Videographers Chuck Sanders and Lynn Chambers were my

camera crew. In our newscruiser, with Sanders driving, we struggled through the icy, blowing snow to the intersection of Rocky River Drive and Brookpark Road. There, the snow became so thick and heavy, the drifts so large, we could go no further.

During brief lulls in the wind I could see one of the lime-green Cleveland Police cruisers stopped just a few hundred feet ahead of us. I told the crew to stay in the warmth of our car, then zipped up my parka, pulled on my gloves, and climbed out to wade through the snow drifts toward the police car. I planned to ask the officers if they had found any stranded motorists.

Just then, the wind increased, and my view of the world turned white. I tried to keep walking forward, figuring I would eventually reach the police car. But as I walked, the drifts were getting deeper and deeper, nearly waist high, and I felt I should have already reached the police vehicle. I stopped and listened, but all I could hear was the screaming of the wind. Because of the heavy snow I could see nothing around me. I couldn't tell if I was on the road or off the highway. I was straining to see something, anything, through the wind-blown snow that would tell me where I was in relation to the police car or my news cruiser. Suddenly I realized I was lost in the snow and that if I stepped into a ditch or curb and fell down, no one would be able to find me.

I frantically started to walk in what I hoped were large circles, hoping to come in contact with the street, a car, a lamp post. Several minutes went by. The numbing cold was starting to seep through my coat and gloves, and I could still see nothing but whiteness everywhere I looked.

Then I heard something. It was a siren and a horn blowing. I followed the sound, and a few minutes later I saw a flashing red light to my right. It was the police car. I had become disoriented in the snow and wandered into a nearby field away from Rocky River Drive and the police car. Lynn Chambers had become con-

On Brookpark Road, near Cleveland Hopkins Airport, police had to go car to car looking for stranded motorists. *(Cleveland Public Library)*

cerned when she saw me disappear into the whiteout. When I didn't return, she had gone to the police car and told the officers the last direction she had seen me walking. The police started blowing their horn and turned on their siren, which literally saved my life.

"It was a challenge to cover the many stories," Virgil Dominic recalls of that unusually busy news day. "I can recall vividly [reporter] Jeff Maynor standing by a bridge that overlooked a highway strewn with cars that were unable to move. Jeff was so bundled up he was almost unrecognizable. But he stood his ground and did a great storytelling job while the snow swept the space between him and the camera. At times he would just disappear as the snow intensified."

By that afternoon, the Ohio Turnpike was closed over its entire length for the first time in its history. Many other interstate highways were also blocked as snow drifts rose higher and higher.

It wasn't just the snow—actually, only six to twelve inches fell during the storm—but the high winds that drove the snow into drifts that in some places were over forty feet high, plus the subzero temperature.

In Dayton, the airport was snowbound and forced to close for the first time in its history. More than 150 travelers were stranded in the terminal.

Small towns and villages all over the state found themselves cut off as the snow continued to pile up, drifting higher and higher. Some roofs collapsed from the weight of the snow that accumulated. The wind knocked down small buildings, trees, and utility poles. By the end of the day, the windchill had sunk to nearly to 50 degrees below zero.

Near Columbus, Ohio state patrol officer Gary Taylor was trying to get his family to his parents' home. Taylor had just been transferred to the West Jefferson Post in Franklin County, and his new apartment had lost its power in the storm and had no heat. Learning that his parents still had electricity and a working furnace, he got his family to their house on the west side of Columbus, then called his post to tell them where he was. The sergeant at the West Jefferson Post asked if he could make it to the post, even if he didn't have his uniform with him. Only two troopers had been able to get into work through the storm. The patrol post was being swamped by calls for assistance. Cars with families in them were snowbound on the interstate highways. U.S. Route 40 was impassable, and trucks and cars were being abandoned in snow drifts. Overwhelmed police departments in the Columbus suburbs were asking for help with accidents, blocked roads, and abandoned cars. Taylor strapped on his gun belt, pinned his badge to the front of the winter parka he was wearing, and set off for the patrol post.

In southwestern Ohio, snowplows created walls of snow in their efforts to keep the roads open during the storm. *(Courtesy of the Ohio State Highway Patrol)*

Back at the WJW-TV station in Cleveland, Virgil Dominic recalls, "I left the station at 10 p.m. thinking I could get home in time to watch our 11 p.m. news show. I took Martin Luther King Jr. Drive and got as far as University Circle. There, I encountered the biggest traffic jam I had ever seen. Cars were everywhere, and they had completely stopped. They were filled with people who worked downtown. They had left their offices in late afternoon to go home, but at nearly 11 o'clock at night they were completely stymied. A graveyard of cars, their lights trying to pierce the storm. They were stretched all the way down Chester and Euclid to Public Square. It was an amazing sight. I managed to get turned around and make it back to the station."

In West Jefferson, Gary Taylor had reached patrol post 49 and was told to lead a convoy onto the interstate highway to help stranded motorists.

"We had a patrol car and a National Guard deuce and a half, those big troop-carrying trucks that followed us around as we went onto U.S. 40 where we found several snowbound cars with people inside," he recalled. "We would load the people into the back of the truck where they had blankets to wrap up in and take them to the West Jefferson Police Department where they had some heat and power." Taylor spent the entire night rescuing people from cars that became bogged down on U.S. 40 and on I-70.

By nightfall, the governor's office in Columbus said that upwards of 200,000 Ohio homes and businesses had lost electric power. The governor ordered that all National Guard armories in the state be opened as shelters for those who needed a warm place to ride out the storm.

In Cleveland, videographers Bill Wolfe and Chuck Sanders had been assigned to go with me out to the armory in Brookpark to see how many people were in need there and how they were doing.

We traveled down the nearly deserted Pearl Road, which has only a single lane open to traffic in either direction. It was so cold out that with three people in the news cruiser, the moisture from our collective breathing was coating the windows of the car with a layer of ice. Then the car suddenly lurched. We had blown our left front tire.

With a wind chill around 50 below zero, none of us wanted to attempt to change a tire in the middle of a blizzard, so we kept driving on the flat tire looking for a garage that might be open. We found one, but the attendant pointed to his full garage and said he had lost power and was closing because he had no heat. So we continued to drive on the flat tire south on Pearl Road, hoping to find another garage. When we reached the Snow Road intersection, we began to see sparks coming from the front of the car. The tire had shredded, and we were now driving on the steel wheel rim. It was also at this point that we realized our two-way radio had stopped working. We needed to find a telephone so we could call for assistance.

The Bit of Budapest Restaurant was just ahead of us. When we reached the driveway, the parking lot was empty and all the lights were off, but with a shower of sparks we pulled into the snowdrift-clogged parking lot anyway. Johnny Tarr, the owner of the restaurant, was a close friend, and I knew he lived in a small brick home behind the restaurant.

The three of us, myself, Wolfe, and Sanders, struggled through the drifts to the front door of the house. There were lights on. We pounded on the door. Waited. Pounded again and waited some more. We were beginning to fear that no one was home when the door was opened by John Tarr's wife, Lisa. She was wearing a negligee, and John was just buttoning up his shirt. It was obvious that we had interrupted a romantic snowbound evening.

They were very gracious and invited the three of us, now snow-covered and shivering, into their home. John went next door to the kitchen of the restaurant and brought back a steaming pot of soup while Lisa poured cup after cup of hot coffee. It was the first warm food the three of us had had all day.

While we were warming up, I called the station on Tarr's telephone and explained what had happened. They dispatched chief photographer Cook Goodwin to pick us up in another news cruiser.

We continued our mission to the National Guard Armory, where we interviewed several stranded motorists and guard officers. Then, we fought our way back through the storm to the TV station in time for the 11 p.m. news broadcast.

Virgil Dominic recalls: "We stayed on the air all night long, breaking into regular programming with the latest news. At that late hour the station was still jammed with our fellow employ-

For the first time in its history, the Ohio Turnpike was shut down across the state because of the high winds and drifting snow. *(Courtesy of the Ohio State Highway Patrol)*

ees. No one could return home. By that time all of us were at the point of exhaustion. I went to our security guard and had him open our third-floor conference room. A gang of us went up there and rearranged the furniture so our people could sleep on the chairs and sofas and on the floor which, thank goodness, was carpeted. I called our general manager Bill Flynn, who was at home, and asked permission to open the bar. We put out bourbon and scotch for anyone who needed a nightcap in order to sleep."

At our station on the shores of Lake Erie, the winds blew across Lake Erie and assaulted our building all night long. You could hear it smashing into the windows with loud howls. As dawn came, the storm had abated a bit, and there were periods of sun, but the city remained paralyzed.

Rescue workers, the day after the storm, had to literally dig out buried trucks while looking for survivors along U.S. Route 40. *(Courtesy of the Ohio State Highway Patrol)*

It would take days for things to start to return to normal and even weeks before the full extent of the storm would be realized.

Afterward . . .

In Marion, Ohio, Mary Ellen Withrow, after being snowbound for several days, learned that a neighbor at the end of her road still had electric power and a working telephone. She asked a neighbor across the road, Joe Criswell, if he would fire up his big farm tractor and take her and daughter Becky to the house on the corner that still had power. He agreed, so mother and daughter, wrapped head-to-toe in blankets, perched precariously on the back of the big orange Case tractor, bounced and plowed their way through deep snow drifts to the neighbor's home where Mary Ellen said, "It was warm, and I drank cup after cup of hot coffee."

Across the state a total of fifty-one people had died as a result of the storm. Twenty-two people lost their lives because they walked away from their stranded vehicle to seek shelter and never made it. Thirteen people froze to death inside their vehicles. Thirteen people died in unheated homes. Two people died in the collapse of a building, and one died of unspecified causes.

One of the more amazing stories to come out of the Blizzard of 1978 was that of 42-year-old Cleveland truck driver James Truly.

In an interview for WJW-TV at the time, Truly told me he had left Cleveland on the day the blizzard began, hauling a load of steel coils to the Fisher Body Plant in Mansfield. His wife had warned him during a phone call earlier that day that the television was saying the area was going to be hit by a blizzard, but he told her he thought he could beat the storm and return home.

As he was driving on Ohio Route 13 near Mansfield, he said, "The storm had become so bad I just couldn't see anywhere. I couldn't see the road; I had to stop."

The snow quickly began to drift around his stopped truck, the wind piling it up to the tops of the wheels and then even higher.

Truly had a citizen's band, or CB, radio on, which he had used earlier to chat with another CB user in Mansfield. But the transmit function had stopped working on his radio, and now he could only listen to other people talking.

The situation got worse. The blowing snow had now covered his truck, and when it covered the exhaust pipes, his truck stalled and would not start again. Now he had no heat.

Even though it was still daytime, Truly noticed it was getting darker inside his freezing truck. He tried to open the cab door but could not. It was frozen shut and covered with deep snow. His truck was disappearing into a snow drift.

Truly was able to roll down the window and, using a safety

helmet he had in the truck, he scooped some snow and brought it inside to melt for water to drink.

His truck cab was a "sleeper" unit, meaning it had a bunk behind the driver's seat. He had one blanket with him, and there were some curtains to wall off the bunk. He took the curtains down, wrapped his feet in them, then covered himself with the blanket and settled down to wait to be rescued. What Truly didn't know is that it would be nearly a week until he would be found.

When Truly did not show up or call his family after the storm ended, they became concerned and started looking for him.

Truly, trapped in the dark of the freezing cab of his truck inside a giant snow drift, wasn't sure whether it was night or day. He said he heard the sounds of occasional snowmobiles and even airplanes. But no one came to help him.

He said he prayed a lot and moved around the cab to try to get warm. But he never lost hope. His brother, Donald, of Parma, knew where he was going, and he felt certain his brother would find him.

In fact, Donald was looking for him. On their sixth day of searching, Donald and his nephew, Eugene Jasper, also of Parma, had retraced Donald Truly's route to Mansfield. While travelling down Ohio Route 13, Donald noticed the huge snow drift—and something else. When he climbed the drift, he saw a tiny silver top of a CB antenna sticking out of the snow.

Underneath the snow, inside his frozen truck, James Truly heard voices and started yelling and beating on the roof of the cab with a piece of pipe he found on the floor.

Within minutes, Donald and Eugene had dug down to the cab and could look in the now-open window. "There was my brother," Donald said.

"I knew he wouldn't give up until he found me," James Truly said.

They took Truly to Mansfield Hospital, where he walked into the emergency room in high spirits. Other than being hungry and tired, he was fine. He was released by the hospital and went home that evening.

For those who lived through it, the "Blizzard of '78" became the storm by which to measure all other winter storms.

Virgil Dominic went on to have a long and distinguished career in Cleveland television and retired in 1995.

Joseph Tegreene left politics to become an attorney and shares his time between Cleveland and Florida.

Mayor Dennis Kucinich went on to serve many years in Congress and even ran for president of the United States.

Officer Gary Taylor had a long career with the Ohio State Highway Patrol and retired as a staff lieutenant.

John London, the young WLW reporter who walked through a blizzard to spend hours reporting on the storm, went on to become a Cincinnati broadcasting icon, and as of this writing is still reporting for WLW-TV.

Mary Ellen Withrow was relieved to learn that the county's tax bills were delivered after the storm. She went on to be elected to two terms as treasurer of the state of Ohio, and in 1994 was appointed 40th treasurer of the United States by President Clinton. She held that post until 2001.

James Truly passed away in 1986.

The Silver Bridge Collapse

IT WAS A Christmastime nightmare.

December 15, 1967, just ten days until Christmas. It was early evening, and the streets in this small Southern Ohio community were crowded. Families were Christmas shopping, and it was also the end of the workday, so many people were headed home.

Kanauga, Ohio, is just a dot on the map. A tiny, unincorporated community outside the county seat of Gallipolis that sits on the bank of the Ohio River, across from Point Pleasant, West Virginia.

A 1,750-foot-long bridge carried people and material across the deep waters of the Ohio River between the two states. It was called the Silver Bridge because of its paint job. Built in 1928, it was a unique eye-bar chain suspension bridge, strung from towers on both sides of the river. It soared 102 feet above the river's surface.

The span had been built to carry US Route 35 across the river.

That evening it was bumper-to-bumper traffic on the bridge as cars and trucks hurried home from work or a day of Christmas shopping.

Then, at about 5 p.m., the unthinkable happened.

Charlene Foster, who lived in Kanauga on the edge of the river, in sight of the bridge, told the *Gallipolis Daily Tribune* that she was preparing dinner in the kitchen of her home when her two sons suddenly screamed, "Mommy! Mommy! The bridge is in the water." She looked toward the bridge, and "It was just like a snake slithering down into the water. It seemed to go down in slow-motion."

Ann Davis, who worked in a beverage store near the bridge, was watching the heavy traffic cross the bridge when she heard a large boom. She told the *Plain Dealer* that it sounded like a sonic boom, and then "the bridge started to crumple and sink like a set of dominoes falling. Cars were being crushed like toys in the girders."

It took just twenty seconds for the entire bridge to fall into the river.

Cecil Newell, 24, worked as an orderly at Holzer Hospital in Gallipolis. The *Plain Dealer* reported that he was on the West Virginia side of the river, headed for work and only two car-lengths from getting on the bridge when the structure collapsed in front of him. "The car started vibrating, there was an awful noise, I went out and looked. There were all kinds of cars floating, then everything was so quiet, like nothing had happened, but I knew I had seen it. People were down there in the water."

Charlene Clark Wood of Gallipolis had just finished the day working at a hair salon. She was pregnant and tired. She had driven across the bridge to check on her parents who lived in Point Pleasant and was now heading back home to Ohio. She was driving her brand new 1967 Pontiac. She told the Huntington (WV) *Herald-Dispatch*, "As I was approaching the bridge when the light changed. When it went to green, I started over the bridge and there was a terrible shaking of the bridge." Wood said, "My father was a riverboat captain and had talked about barges hitting the bridge and the pier. So when I heard that sound, I automatically put my car in reverse. By the time I got my car stopped, mine was on the very edge of where the bridge broke off."

The bridge surface she had been on just seconds before was

Cars and trucks were trapped by falling steel girders at each end of the bridge as it collapsed. *(Courtesy of the Ohio State Highway Patrol)*

gone. Only her quick action had saved her life. Wood recalls seeing wires dangling, and she remembered a state patrol officer, Rudy Odell, and a volunteer, later identified as Robert Rimmey, coming to her car and walking her off the bridge. "You could hear people screaming," she said. "It was terrible. By the time I went to the end of the bridge, I had gone into shock."

Ruth Fout, co-author of the book *The Silver Bridge Disaster of 1967* and administrative assistant at the Point Pleasant River Museum and Learning Center, recalls that a few cars did not fall into the water but were trapped on what was left of the bridge by tons of falling steel girders. "Melvin and Margaret Mae Cantrell, along with their friend, Cecil Clyde Counts, were headed for town when the bridge fell. Mrs. Cantrell was driving. A steel beam crashed onto their car, pinning it to the bridge. Melvin

Cantrell, who was in the front passenger seat, and Cecil Counts, who was in the back seat, were both killed. Rescue workers were able to pull Margaret Cantrell from the wreckage. She survived."

It was just a few minutes before police, fire, and other rescue workers started arriving on both sides of the river. But there was little they could do. Many vehicles had sunk beneath the waters, and others were tangled in tons of twisted steel that had collapsed on top of the vehicles in the river. Several small boats were launched to search for survivors.

One of the first pulled from the icy river waters was 24-year-old Howard Boggs of Bidwell, Ohio. He and his wife, 18-year-old Marjorie, and their 17-month-old daughter, had just started across the bridge when it collapsed. "That old bridge was bouncing up and down like it always does," he told the *Cincinnati Enquirer*. "Then, all of a sudden everything was falling down. My feet touched the damned bottom of the river. I don't know how I came up. I must have blacked out again, because the next thing I knew I was hanging onto this barrel." He sobbed, "I just hope to God that Marjorie and the baby got out OK."

Local law enforcement officials had no idea of just how many cars and trucks had plunged into the river. They estimated the loss could go as high as 100. The Ohio River at that point is about 30 to 70 feet deep, and there are strong currents.

One of the first reporters on the scene was 20-year-old Rondal "Ron" Akers for WCMI radio, the CBS affiliate in Huntington, West Virginia. He recalls that there were no police barricades, and he was able to pull right up to the edge of where the bridge used to be on the Point Pleasant side of the river. He was "gobsmacked" by the sight before him. "When the bridge collapsed, it twisted upon itself and the cars were tangled in the superstructure of the bridge," he said. "It was kind of like wringing out a cloth. There was a car that was squished down so it looked like it was two feet across."

Pieces of twisted steel can be seen in the Ohio River, marking the spot where the Silver Bridge collapsed into the Ohio River on December 15, 1967, killing forty-six people. *(Courtesy of the Ohio State Highway Patrol)*

William Edmondson, 38, of North Carolina, told the *Cincinnati Enquirer* he was driving a large tractor-trailer across the bridge when the bridge suddenly collapsed. "Traffic was bumper-to-bumper, about three feet apart. It was backed up from a red light on the Ohio side. I was in the right lane, going north, the bridge came loose on the right side first, the side I was on. The bridge rolled over . . . . I felt it settling down. It was like an elevator, but fast. . . . It felt like rock when we hit the water. My truck was on its right side, and it instantly filled with water, although the windows were up. I thought I was a goner. I didn't think it was possible I could get out of the vehicle, but then the door tore off on my side and I floated out. I started floating towards the surface and then I started paddling."

Edmondson swam to a roll of rubber fabric, cargo from his

truck, and held on until a boat reached him. He had been in the frigid waters for about ten minutes.

William M. Needham, 27, also of North Carolina, had a similar brush with death. He told the *Gallipolis Daily Tribune* that when his truck crashed into the river, it "sank like a rock. We went all the way to the bottom. The windows were up. I held my breath, I reached for the handle of the window, but I couldn't find it. I was able to get my fingers in a small crack at the top of the window. I pulled the window down that way and got out." Needham swam to the surface and was picked up by rescuers. "I wanted to make it home for Christmas," he said from his hospital bed. "But, I'm happy to just be alive. I'm a very lucky man."

Not so lucky was his driving partner and alternate driver, R. E. Towe, who was asleep in the cab when the span fell and was now among the missing. His body would later be found.

Paul Scott, 52, of Middleport, was another who survived the crash into the river. He recalls that he and fellow passenger Frederick "Dean" Miller of Gallipolis were riding in a car driven by James Pullen of Middleport. They had reached the high middle of the bridge, and Scott was looking out the window when "the bridge began shaking." Then, the side of the bridge they were on collapsed. "I remember it going down," Scott said, "but I don't remember how I got out. The next thing I knew, I was struggling towards the surface in the cold water. It seemed like forever before I was rescued by a boat."

Pullen and Mitchell did not make it out of the sunken car.

Radio reporter Ron Akers was interviewing a Point Pleasant police officer at the edge of the bridge. "It was incredibly cold that night," he recalls. "All I had on was a sports coat. I tell you, it was cold. Suddenly he [the officer] stopped and said, '*Listen. Listen.*' There was a male voice calling for help. We couldn't see him. I don't know if they ever found him."

The access road to the bridge also proved to be a trap for many cars and trucks as the bridge went tumbling into the river. *(Courtesy of the Ohio State Highway Patrol)*

No barge-mounted heavy cranes were immediately available to use as rescue equipment. Portable cranes brought to the river's edge were just not powerful enough to lift heavy, water-filled cars to the surface.

A large tow truck tried to pull a car out of the water near the bridge, but the weight was too great, and the tow truck ripped the steering mechanism and wheels off the car.

By the time darkness fell, hundreds of people had gathered on the banks of the river. Coast Guard boats had joined the volunteers in private boats searching the dark waters. Dozens of volunteer divers were arriving.

Tim Jameson, 26, a gas station attendant in Point Pleasant, put on his diving gear and went shivering onto the dark river water among the twisted steel beams. But he had to stop because it was too dangerous to go further in the dark. He could see two people trapped in a car under a beam. The car was crushed; the couple pinned inside were dead.

"You can see them, if you duck down, a man and a woman," he told the *Plain Dealer*. "I'd give anything to go in there and get them out, not because it would help them any, but it's, well, it's proper. A human being deserves something better than that even if it's dead. I'm going home now and tomorrow morning at dawn I'm going to come back here and get down there and get some of these people out. It's the least I can do. I may have friends down there. I don't know."

The *Gallipolis Daily Tribune* reported that, as of midnight on that terrible day, there were so far a total of four known dead and at least eleven survivors who were patients at Holzer Hospital in Gallipolis. Across the river in Pleasant Valley Hospital were six survivors. Rescue workers were still struggling to determine just how many people had been on the bridge when it collapsed and how many of those people were still missing.

Automobiles and trucks lined up along the riverbanks so their headlights could help illuminate the dark river waters. Floodlights were mounted to trees and to some of the bridge wreckage to give rescue workers light to work by. Local phone service was overwhelmed as lines were jammed by hundreds of people frantically calling loved ones to learn if they were safe. Police were trying to compile lists of people whom anxious relatives and friends thought might have been on the bridge when it went down.

As the night went on, authorities realized that anyone still in the water was probably dead, either from the fall into the river or by drowning. Even if they survived and somehow reached the surface, unless rescued immediately they probably would have perished within an hour from hypothermia in the cold river.

All night long, radio reporter Ron Akers huddled whenever

An unidentified Ohio State Highway patrol trooper stands at what was once the roadway onto the Silver Bridge that connected Ohio and West Virginia. *(Courtesy of the Ohio State Highway Patrol)*

he could in a phone booth near the bridge to keep warm and to file reports with his radio station in Huntington, which in turn forwarded his reports to the CBS network.

By dawn, the search and rescue operation had ended. Now, it became a recovery mission.

The United States Army Corps of Engineers arrived with five barge-mounted cranes.

Professional divers were arriving with their equipment. However, when the divers donned their bulky suits and helmets, attached to air hoses, and entered the river, they were hampered by the swift current and the fact that recent heavy rains had swollen the river and made the water too murky to see anything.

After surfacing from one dive, Max Ray, a deep-sea diver

from New Orleans, told the *Plain Dealer*, "It's hairy and dangerous down there. You've got to worry about metal falling on you. I dropped through that mess, and it started to slide. It's so shaky, I could move those beams with my hand. You can't see your hand on the faceplate of your mask."

Nevertheless, Ray and his fellow divers, joined by some scuba divers, made repeated dives into the darkness of the river, using their hands to feel for wrecked cars and victims.

By Sunday morning, divers had located several cars and trucks underwater and were able to attach cables to the wreckage, enabling the barge cranes to pull them out of the river.

It was a slow process. By the end of the day, they had recovered eight bodies.

Most of the people still missing were assumed to be in the river. People like Lee "Doc" Otto Sanders, who drove the local taxi. Sanders was not supposed to be working that evening, but when another driver called off, Sanders took a passenger, Ronald Gene Moore, who wanted to go to Point Pleasant. The two were on the bridge when it collapsed.

Thomas Allen Cantrell (no relation to Melvin Cantrell, also killed on the bridge) was a newspaper delivery man. He intended to quit his job that day and had plans to go to California and become a cartoonist. He had made his last run to deliver papers to Point Pleasant and was on his way back to Gallipolis to drop off his keys when the bridge fell.

A good deed apparently cost Ronald Robert Sims his life. He left work late from his job as a designer at the Goodyear plant in order to give Bobby Head a ride home. They were on the bridge when it went down.

The list of missing persons contained names of men, women, and children—in some cases, several members of the same family.

State trooper Rudy Odell had been assigned the terrible job

The U.S. Army Corps of Engineers brought in barge-mounted cranes to bring up submerged cars and trucks that were tangled in steel girders of the wreckage of the downed bridge in the river bottom. *(Courtesy of the Ohio State Highway Patrol)*

of tagging each victim pulled from the water before the body was taken to a temporary morgue.

The grief felt by each of the families and loved ones of the victims is beyond anyone's ability to describe or understand. And the effects would be long lasting. In some cases, the family breadwinner had perished, forcing many families to face hardship in the months and years to come.

The recovery of the bodies was painfully slow. It would be almost six months after the collapse of the bridge when the last known body was recovered, found by fishermen downriver. It was finally determined that forty-six people had been killed in the tragedy.

Two victims were never recovered.

According to Ruth Fout, Catherine Lucille Byus was ten years old and riding with her two-month-old sister, Kimberly, and their mother, Hilda. All three were killed. The bodies of Hilda and baby Kimberly were found downriver several weeks after the collapse of the bridge. Catherine's body was never found.

Maxine Turner of Point Pleasant was riding with her husband, Victor. They had just gone to Gallipolis to pick up her niece and were headed back home when the tragedy occurred. The bodies of her husband and niece were recovered, but Maxine's was never found.

Within hours of the bridge collapse, the National Transportation Safety Board launched an investigation into its cause. Along with the cars and trucks recovered from the river, divers and cranes brought up the tangled steel that was once the bridge. Investigators used a field nearby to loosely reassemble the bridge in their search for clues.

After nearly three and half years of investigation, the board finally released its findings in April 1971. The cause, the report said, was "a cleavage fracture in the lower limb of the eye of eyebar 330 at joint C13N of the north eyebar suspension chain in the Ohio side span. The fracture was caused by the development of a critical size flaw over the 40-year life of the structure as the result of the joint action of stress corrosion and corrosion fatigue."

The report also stated that the corroded part that fractured and caused the collapse was in a place impossible to see unless the bridge had been dismantled.

A new bridge, the Silver Memorial Bridge, was built about a mile south of the original location, between Gallipolis and Henderson, West Virginia. It was opened to traffic exactly two years to the day the original bridge fell, December 15, 1969.

The new bridge, unlike the failed Silver Bridge, is a cantilever-styled crossing—meaning support is required on only one side of each cantilever—which is considered a much safer bridge for heavy traffic.

The Silver Bridge disaster also brought about new federal laws regarding inspections and, perhaps most important, load limits for bridges. (There were no load limits in 1967.)

A couple of bright spots appeared during my research of this terrible tragedy.

On December 30th, 1967, just fifteen days after the fall of the bridge—fifteen days after Paul A. Scott was riding in a car that sank to the bottom of the Ohio River, killing two of his companions—Scott, with his arm still bandaged from his ordeal, walked his daughter, Carol, down the aisle at her wedding.

And remember Charlene Clark Wood, the quick-thinking pregnant woman who saved her own life by driving in reverse on the falling bridge? Just four months later, in April 1968, she gave birth to twins, a boy and a girl.

Radio reporter Ron Akers of WCMI left broadcasting to become a member of the Ohio state patrol. Then after six years of that, he decided to become a doctor. So he went back to school and eventually became Dr. Rondal Akers. He practiced in Cleveland, Tennessee, until his retirement.

Today, at the end of Sixth Street in Point Pleasant, where the approach to the Silver Bridge once stood, there is a brickwork memorial with forty-six names:

Albert A. Adler, Jr., Gallipolis, Ohio	Donna Jean Casey, Gallipolis, Ohio
J.O. Bennett, Walnut Cove, N.C.	Cecil Counts, Gallipolis Ferry, W.Va.
Leo Blackman, Richmond, Va.	Horace Cremeans, Gallipolis, Ohio
Kristye Boggs, Vinton, Ohio	Harold Cundiff, Winston-Salem, NC
Margaret Boggs, Vinton, Ohio	Alonzo Luther Darst, Cheshire, Ohio
Hilda Byus, Point Pleasant, W.Va.	Alma Duff, Point Pleasant, W.Va.
Kimberly Byus, Point Pleasant, W.Va.	James Hawkins, Westerville, Ohio
Melvin Cantrell, Gallipolis Ferry, W.Va.	Bobby L. Head, Gallipolis, Ohio
Thomas A. Cantrell, Gallipolis, Ohio	Forrest Raymond Higley, Bidwell, Ohio

Alva B. Lane, Gallipolis, Ohio

Thomas "Bus" Howard Lee, Gallipolis, Ohio

G. H. Mabe, Jamestown, NC

Darlene Mayes, Kanauga, Ohio

Gerald G. McMannus, South Point, Ohio

James Richard Maxwell, Gallipolis, Ohio

James F. Meadows, Point Pleasant, W.Va.

Timothy Meadows, Point Pleasant, W.Va.

Frederick D. Miller, Gallipolis, Ohio

Ronnie G. Moore, Gallipolis, Ohio

Nora Isabelle Nibert, Gallipolis Ferry, W.Va.

Darius E. Northup, Gallipolis Ferry, W.Va.

James O. Pullen, Middleport, Ohio

Leo "Doc" Sanders, Point Pleasant, W.Va.

Ronald Sims, Gallipolis, Ohio

Charles T. Smith, Bidwell, Ohio

Oma Mae Smith, Bidwell, Ohio

Maxine Sturgeon, Kanauga, Ohio

Denzil Taylor, Point Pleasant, W.Va.

Glenna Mae Taylor, Point Pleasant, W.Va.

Robert Eugene Towe, Cana, Va.

Victor William Turner, Point Pleasant, W.Va.

Marvin Wamsley, Point Pleasant, W.Va.

Lillian Eleanor Wedge, Point Pleasant, W.Va.

Paul D. Wedge, Point Pleasant, W.Va.

James Alfred White, Point Pleasant, W.Va.

Kathy Byus, Point Pleasant, W.Va.

Maxine Turner, Point Pleasant W.Va.

Forty-six people who, on December 15, 1967, crossed the Silver Bridge into eternity.

The Cleveland Circus Fire

DURING MY REPORTER days at WJW-TV I did a lot of feature stories. My assignment editor Neil "Mickey" Flanagan knew that I was not particularly fond of animals—especially animals bigger than I am, such as elephants—so he enjoyed making sure I got all the assignments for stories about animals. And whenever the circus was in town, he would arrange for me to ride an elephant for a story.

It was sometime in the 1970s when Ringling Bros. and Barnum & Bailey Circus came to the Cleveland-Akron area and I was assigned to meet the circus train in the tiny town of Peninsula, south of Cleveland, to ride one of their elephants from the train to the nearby Richfield Coliseum, where the circus was having a four-day run. While plodding along on the top of a ten-foot-high elephant, I struck up a conversation with the elephant's handler, a middle-aged man who told me he had been with the circus for nearly thirty years. He asked me if I knew about the big fire in Cleveland that nearly wiped out the circus during World War II back in the 1940s. I had not. But I promised that I would look it up, and maybe someday do a story about the fire.

Today is the day.

August 4th, 1942, was a typical summer day in Cleveland according to my friend and former colleague, WJW-TV meteorologist Andre Bernier. The temperature would hit 80 degrees.

Hopkins Airport had recorded a few light showers, but for a city still reeling from the start of World War II just eight months earlier, it was the kind of day that made you not think about your problems. It was one of those perfect days you recall when you think of summer.

The Ringling Bros. and Barnum & Bailey Circus was in Cleveland on the second day of a four-day run.

It had not been a good year for the circus. Tragedy had struck just nine months earlier when eleven of their elephants died while the show was in Atlanta, Georgia. They had consumed large amounts of arsenic, and an investigation into just who had given it to them was still going on. (No one was ever charged with the crime.) The circus was short-handed, too. The war was siphoning off many of the workers who used to be attracted to the adventure of the big top.

A whole series of giant red and blue circus tents had been set up on the northeast corner of East Ninth Street and Lakeside Avenue. In addition to the tents, the circus train had brought to town 1,009 animals ranging from elephants to zebras, and over 800 performers and crew. Once all was set up, this was a virtual city of exotic entertainment, all under canvas. The main feature this year was an elephant ballet starring many of the fifty elephants that traveled with the show.

Early on August 4, Walter McClain, the circus's longtime chief handler of elephants, was overseeing the morning care of the herd of pachyderms.

Not far from the circus grounds, at East Thirteenth Street and Rockwell Avenue, were the barns of the Cleveland Police Mounted Unit. Patrolman Anthony (Tony) E. Welling was on his mount, "Skippy," a big Morgan horse, and was just starting daily patrol of the lakefront area.

Farther west on Lakeside Avenue, Chester Koch, a World War I veteran who had been named Cleveland's director of patriotic activities, was meeting with armed forces recruiters attempting to arrange free circus tickets for those men about to leave for military training.

William O. Walker, editor of the *Call and Post*, was at the circus ticket wagon getting ready to purchase some tickets for the day's matinee that he was going to use to reward youngsters who delivered the newspaper.

Before the day was over, all of these people—and many others— would have a role in the tragedy that was about to unfold.

In the late morning, "cage boys"—a circus term for young men who cared for the many animals in the circus—and other circus laborers had been pushing wheelbarrows full of bloody chunks of meat from cage to cage to feed the lions, tigers, and other meat-eating big cats. Other workers spread fresh hay and grain for elephants and horses. New straw bedding was also forked into each animal enclosure. There were fifty elephants staked around the giant menagerie tent, along with a host of camels, giraffes, assorted animal cages, and a herd of horses.

At 11:15 a.m. a flag went up on the cook tent, located across the street at the other end of the midway. It signified that lunch was now being served for the circus workers. This was the last chance to get something to eat before the afternoon matinee performance that would begin around 1 p.m. So, with their charges munching and grazing away, the cage boys joined the other circus workers wending their way to the tent-kitchen, where long tables were set up to feed the workers.

Just as the group was sitting down, according to a story reported by the *Plain Dealer*, someone yelled, "Fire!"

Other people took up the cry as all eyes turned across the street, where flames were leaping and smoke was billowing above the huge 320-foot-long and 120-foot-wide menagerie tent that held the majority of the circus animals.

There was sudden chaos. Everyone was shouting and running

toward the fire. According to a *Cleveland Press* article, some witnesses described it like "a tidal wave of orange" as the flames spread across the tent that was the size of a football field.

Patrolman Tony Welling and Skippy had been on Lakeside and had just turned south on East Twelfth Street when Skippy pricked up his ears at hearing the commotion and nervously turned around. Welling saw the flames and spurred Skippy forward. Within seconds, the big horse was galloping down Lakeside, his hooves sounding like drum beats on the pavement. As horse and rider came onto the circus lot, bits of flaming canvas were already floating from the sky and dropping onto the rescue workers who were starting to arrive. Welling urged Skippy into the burning tent, and the well-trained police horse did as commanded.

In an interview years later in the *Lake County Herald*, Welling recalled, "I spotted a tent with horses inside, so I went inside and grabbed the lead mare and the other horses followed her as I led them out." Twenty circus horses followed Skippy through the smoke and fire out of the tent. Welling and another Cleveland patrolman, Bill Carter, were able to move the horses to a nearby vacant lot, where they kept them corralled until circus workers came to take charge of the animals. Welling said he got a little "singed" by the fire, and Skippy's fetlocks (the hairy area just above the hooves) got burned, but not seriously.

With the rescue operation now in full swing, according to the *Plain Dealer*, veteran elephant boss Walter McClain led his crew of animal handlers into the flaming tent despite the burning pieces of canvas that were raining down on the animals and the ground—and torching the fresh hay, straw, and sawdust piled throughout the tent.

Fifty elephants were chained to the ground in the tent. Highly disciplined, most of them stood nervously waiting for their trainers to help them. McClain and his men, working in

The fire, fed by the paraffin-soaked canvas of the Big Top, destroyed the menagerie tent, killing dozens of circus animals including elephants. Many of the animals had to be shot by Cleveland Police to end their misery. *(Cleveland Police Historical Society and Museum)*

choking heat and smoke, frantically released each elephant from its chains and then gave the command for them to orderly march out of the flaming embers of their tent.

They had rescued forty-six elephants. But not all of them.

Many other animals were trapped in their cages. Among them were a pair of lions and two tigers. Another enclosure held three giraffes; two died, overcome by the fire and smoke, while one was able to somehow leap over the fencing run into the circus yard filled with rescue workers.

Rescuers tried frantically to get ten camels that were tied together out of the burning tent, but the camels, frozen with fear, refused to move and had to be abandoned. They died where they stood.

Journalist W. O. Walker witnessed what was happening. He described in the *Call & Post* "an ostrich, with its plumage smoldering, ran out and it took three men to down it on a hillside back of the tent."

Walker was also struck by the reaction of the circus animals to the fire and chaos going on around them: "The complete silence of the animals. No agonizing screams, no anguished roars, just silence in the tent with the crackle of flames."

In just twenty minutes the fire was essentially out. The tent had completely burned away, leaving some dead and some badly injured animals and blackened cage wagons among the smoke and smoldering hay and sawdust.

By this time circus officials had been joined by armed Cleveland Police officers. The police were being asked to handle the grim duty of putting down those animals that had been severely burned and were beyond help.

A large elephant named "Ringling Rosie," who had been loosened by McClain and his men, refused to leave the tent with the other elephants.

Walker watched as she stomped in circles as the fire engulfed her. She was terribly burned; large portions of her hide were scorched and smoldering.

As soon as McClain and his men could reach her, they tried to calm her and chain her down so they could treat her wounds but, maddened by the pain, she snapped the chains and started to run in circles. In the process, one side of McClain's face was burned from hairline to his collar. But even as he was being treated, he continued to direct his men who were trying to subdue Rosie, who had gone berserk and was now a threat to rescue workers.

Cleveland police detective Lloyd Trunk was ordered to try to end Rosie's misery by shooting her. He used his police handgun and shot her between the eyes. She went down but was still

It was a gruesome scene. The bodies of dead animals were lying on smoldering bales of hay while stunned circus workers tried to help the surviving animals. *(Cleveland Public Library)*

breathing. Police superintendent D. L. Cowles, using a Thompson submachine gun, fired a burst of .45 caliber bullets into her body in the area of her heart, and she died.

The *Mansfield News Journal* reported: "A sorrowful figure was John Sabo, 'Boss Animal man' for the circus since 1915. 'I knew all those animals, I knew every trick (they could pull),' he said. 'I couldn't even watch while they were being shot. For me it would be just like shooting a child. If I had to shoot one. I liked them all, like babies.'"

While Cleveland firefighters hosed down the smoldering ruins of the great tent, circus workers and police officers went cage to cage, discovering many animals dead from flames or smoke and others badly burned.

The circus's veterinarian, Dr. J. J. Henderson, directed workers using long brushes dipped in an unguent called foile to reach through the bars and attempt to spread the salve on the animals' burns. In some cages, where animals were beyond help, he would signal the Cleveland police officers to end the animal's suffering with their guns.

Circus officials got a pleasant surprise when they approached the blackened cage wagon holding the only baby hippopotamus that traveled with a circus at that time. The small creature had dived into a water-filled pool in the bottom of the cage wagon and stayed submerged while the flames swept over his cage. He was uninjured.

Meanwhile, some of the elephants that had earlier been rescued from the tent now started to wander off in the confusion. Several were heading west on Lakeside Avenue.

Chester Koch, who had earlier spotted the flames, was at that moment walking on Lakeside in front of Cleveland City Hall. He saw the oncoming group of elephants. "This will gum up traffic. Somebody's got to stop them," he said in a later interview with the *Plain Dealer*. Since no one else was doing anything to halt the herd, Koch decided that somebody was going to have to be him. He ran into the middle of the street toward the fast-approaching elephants.

Although he had no experience with elephants, he did have a silver whistle that he carried ever since his days in World War I. He pulled the whistle out of his pocket and blew it as loudly as he could, then yelled "WHOA!"

The elephants stopped.

Then they started again, but slower this time, until they surrounded him. Koch said he talked softly to them as the elephants gathered around him like some giant football huddle. He said he talked "like a Dutch uncle." He was relieved when minutes later circus elephant handlers arrived and took charge. A circus

Despite the nearly quarter-million-dollar loss of the animals and equipment, circus workers rallied, and the show went on that night. *(Cleveland Public Library)*

official said the elephants likely stopped for Koch because they "were looking for a friendly face," the *Plain Dealer* reported.

Back at the circus grounds, the fire was finally out. As firemen continued to soak smoldering bales of hay and bags of grain, circus officials began determining their loss.

Animals that veterinarians thought had a chance of surviving were taken to a makeshift animal hospital set up in the basement of the nearby Cleveland Public Auditorium.

The *New York Times* reported that at least fifty animals were killed in the blaze, including four elephants, thirteen camels, twelve zebras, four lions, three tigers, a puma, and at least sixteen monkeys. John Ringling North, the owner of the circus, walking through the burned-out tent immediately after the fire, said the loss would exceed $200,000 (which as of this writing would be more than $3 million). He said more than the loss of the money he mourned the fact so many of the animals had to suffer.

The circus, living up to the motto "The show must go on," started immediately cleaning up the burned tent area. It was announced they would hold their regular evening performance. And that evening, an estimated 14,000 people turned out for the show.

Investigators immediately began trying to determine the cause of the fire. At first it was believed that a hot coal or spark from a passing steam locomotive on the nearby Pennsylvania Railroad tracks, which ran just below the circus site, might have been the cause. But there were also reports that a disgruntled circus worker had torched the tinder-dry hay and straw after the trainers finished their morning feeding rounds. The day after the fire, the Pittsburgh *Post Gazette* reported, a 16-year-old in Pittsburgh was picked up and confessed to the crime. Cleveland detectives who traveled to Pittsburgh to question him said he didn't do it and that he had confessed because of mental problems. The cause of the fire was never determined.

Firemen did note that the fire burned so swiftly and so hot because the canvas tent had been treated with paraffin and benzine to make it waterproof. That was a common practice at the time, and one that came back to haunt the circus two years later in Hartford, Connecticut, when a similar fire broke out during a circus show that left 167 people dead (many of them children) and injured more than 700. That fire, coupled with the Cleveland disaster, pretty much spelled the end of the tent circus. Although Ringling Bros. started using a new, supposedly fireproof type of canvas dressing, they were besieged by lawsuits over the next dozen years. In 1956 the tent show was done for sure, and the circus moved indoors, to auditoriums and arenas.

Ringling Bros. went out of business in 2017 after 147 years.

Walter McClain, the elephant trainer who saved forty-six elephants in the Cleveland circus fire, was killed just three months later. While helping unload a circus train for an appearance in Florida in November 1942, according to the *New York Times*, he was crushed to death when one of the cage wagons accidentally rolled off a ramp and pinned him to the ground.

Chester Koch, who stopped the runaway troop of elephants, continued as Cleveland director of patriotic affairs, seeing men and women off to military training for forty-seven years until his death in 1989.

W. O. Walker, the journalist who witnessed the fire, went on to a distinguished career. He became the owner of the *Call and Post* and was active in politics. At the time of his death in 1981, he was being considered by President Ronald Reagan for the post of chairman of the U. S. Civil Rights Commission.

Patrolman Tony Welling continued as an officer in the Cleveland Police Mounted Unit until his retirement in 1972. He spent his last years as an amateur archeologist in Lake County and was honored for his research by Lake Erie College in Painesville before his death in 1991.

Skippy was retired sometime in the 1950s. Sadly, many of the photos and records of the Cleveland Mounted unit were lost in a flooded room at the barns many years ago, so no photo could be found of Skippy.

Detective Lloyd Trunk became the only Cleveland police officer to have this notation in his service record: "Ordered to shoot an elephant, August 4th, 1942."

Because the fire occurred nearly eighty years before the writing of this book, I was unable to locate anyone who participated in the event or even remembered it firsthand. The details in this account came from newspaper stories, including the *Cleveland News*, the *Cleveland Press*, the *Plain Dealer*, the *Call and Post,* the *Mansfield Journal,* the *News-Herald,* and several other newspapers and magazines containing historical reports on the tragedy.

One small mystery remains about the aftermath of the fire: What happened to the bodies of the large and exotic animals? Some reports say they were immediately taken to a rendering plant on Denison Avenue. I found one report that said at least the skeletal remains of the camels that perished in the fire were donated to the Cleveland Museum of Natural History. However, a spokesperson from the museum said via email that they had no record of receiving the camels—or any of the other remains.

The Great Cleveland Balloon Launch Fiasco

IT'S A FACT. Helium-filled balloons have always fascinated people. The gaily colored floating orbs bring out the child in us.

The Cleveland United Way Campaign for 1986 came up with an idea that they hoped would raise funds for the charity as well as help reinvigorate some pride in the city. They wanted to claim a spot in the *Guinness Book of Records*. And to do that, they planned to stage the world's largest release of helium-filled latex balloons.

In December 1985, Cheryle Wills, then president of United Way of Cleveland, was on a trip to California and happened to witness a huge launch of balloons at Disneyland in Anaheim. Disney had decided to mark their 30th anniversary by releasing 1.2 million helium-filled balloons and claiming the title for the largest such launch of balloons in the Guinness book of strange and weird records.

When Wills returned home to Cleveland, she suggested a similar event, a record-breaking balloon launch. Disney had sent 1.2 million balloons floating into the heavens, but Cleveland would launch two million. It would be done to raise funds as well as raise awareness of the charity. The United Way brought in an expert: Treb Heining of Balloons by Treb, the Los Angeles firm that had worked on the Disney spectacular. It specialized in all things to do with helium-filled balloons.

Heining's plan was to build a huge enclosure over parts of Cleveland's Public Square, and then encourage local school students to contribute their labor to inflate about two million colored balloons.

The structure would cover about a city block, 250 by 150 feet, and rise about three stories above Public Square in the shadow of the Terminal Tower. The top of the structure would be covered by a one-piece sheet of netting to contain the inflated balloons.

It would require more than 700,000 cubic feet of helium from five tanker trucks to fill all the balloons. That would be enough helium to inflate two Goodyear blimps.

The launch event, dubbed "Balloonfest," would be Saturday, September 27, 1986.

By early September, the 32-year-old Treb Heining was in town, and work was well underway on the project.

The event organizers hoped to have school children collect money for the balloons to be used in the launch. The kids would sell two balloons for a dollar, and for an extra dollar the contributor could write a message that would be placed inside the balloon before it was inflated. The hope was that the school children would be able to raise a million dollars for the charity.

"It will be the most spectacular thing most people will ever see," Heining told me on September 6 for a news story for WJW-TV. "There is something magical about balloons. There is an emotional release involved that is just hard to put your finger on."

That may be true, but these balloons weren't magical enough to raise a million dollars. As the days counted down to the launch date, it became apparent to the event organizers that the school children's campaign was going to fall short of raising the money required to pay for two million balloons. A decision was made to reduce the number of balloons from 2 million to 1.5 million—still enough to beat the Disney launch record and bring the title home to Cleveland.

The nine-inch balloons, made by the Pioneer Balloon Company of Willard, Ohio, came in seven colors and were supposedly biodegradable.

Construction workers scurried around Public Square erecting the huge balloon enclosure, using construction scaffolding to form the framework.

As the building went up, another concern was raised. The sheer number of balloons, once inflated, would create a large, opaque cloud that would block out light needed by volunteers to continue the inflation work. They couldn't use normal floodlights because those would create too much heat and cause the balloons to burst. Cleveland Electric Illuminating Company came to the rescue by installing some special cool lights.

Everything (with the exception of the reduced number of balloons) seemed to be going as planned. There had been a few letters to the editor of the local newspaper expressing concern for all the litter that would be created when the balloons fell from the sky. But that issue seemed to get little attention in the rush to prepare for the record-breaking launch.

When you release a helium-filled balloon into the sky, what happens depends on the weather. If it is a bright, warm, sunny day, the heat may cause the gas-filled balloons to swell up and burst. If there is little or no wind, the balloons may continue to rise and possibly reach altitudes of nearly 30,000 feet. Then, once past that altitude, atmospheric pressure will cause the helium within the balloon to expand, and the balloon will pop and fall back to earth. Whatever goes up must also come down.

The weather in Cleveland the weekend of September 27 was hot and stormy. On Friday night, September 26, the day before the planned launch, a thunderstorm hit downtown Cleveland, with lots of rain and winds gusting up to sixty miles per hour. Trees and power lines were downed, and more than 5,000 Cleveland residents lost power during the storm.

Balloonfest organizers worried that the wind and stormy weather might delay or even wipe out the balloon launch the next day. They breathed a sigh of relief when the storm passed.

"It was very hairy," Treb Heining told me in an interview at the time. "My crew was just getting ready to turn in. We lost 25 of the big inflatables, and the fabric tore on the enclosure. But all in all the structure got no heavy damage."

The storm caused another problem.

Two fishermen, 39-year-old Bernard Sulzer and 40-year-old Raymond Broderick, who were also neighbors, had decided to go fishing Friday night and were in a 16-foot aluminum boat anchored in the lake just west of the breakwall near Edgewater Park when the storm hit. When they did not return home by midnight, family and friends became concerned and started searching for them. By early Saturday morning, both were reported to police as missing.

I was working as a reporter-producer for WJW-TV that day, and when I reported for work Saturday morning, my camera crew and I were dispatched to the U.S. Coast Guard Station on East Ninth Street to report on the search for the two men.

Their boat had been found, still anchored near the breakwall. A pair of tennis shoes and life jackets were floating near the capsized boat. Divers from the Cleveland Police Department were on the scene as were units from the United States Coast Guard. Authorities speculated that the storm might have capsized the fisherman's boat, and then they might have tried to swim to the breakwall or been blown farther out into the lake by the winds. The Coast Guard decided to call in a helicopter to aid in the search.

Although the search was going strong, there was no sign of

It was an amazing sight. Nearly 1.5 million multicolored helium-filled balloons—a world record—were released from Cleveland's Public Square on September 27, 1986. *(Courtesy of Michael Polly)*

the missing men. Shortly after 1 p.m., because I was the only reporter working that weekend at WJW-TV, my pager started to buzz. This was before we had cell phones. I had to seek out a telephone and call the TV station. Since the missing fishermen still had not been found, I was told to break off temporarily from the search story and head downtown to cover the balloon launch, which was scheduled for 2:06 p.m.

Launch day had started at 2 a.m. for 150 volunteers from the Pioneer Balloon Company in Willard. They boarded buses to head for Cleveland to help inflate the million and a half balloons. Starting at 4 a.m., students, nearly 2,500 of them from schools all over Greater Cleveland, started arriving at Public Square.

There, while being entertained by clowns and rock music from local station WMMS-FM, blasting from a portable studio set up on the northwest quadrant of Public Square, the volunteers were rapidly filling balloons with helium. Four hundred helium lines snaked from the five tanker trucks into the huge balloon enclosure. Four students or volunteers worked on each line, inflating, tying off, and releasing balloons, one by one, into the enclosure. Each volunteer was trying to average three to four balloons per minute.

By 1 p.m. the crowd of nearly 100,000 spectators had gathered on the streets and sidewalks around Public Square. It was wall-to-wall people crowding in around the several thousand workers who were frantically inflating balloons—and sweating. The humidity was rising, and to the west storm clouds were starting to gather.

The National Weather Service had issued a forecast for that day that included the possibility of severe thunderstorms.

Anxious festival officials huddled. Their target of 1.5 million balloons was supposed to be reached at 2:06 p.m., but with the storm approaching, they decided to launch earlier and cut

Organizers of the balloon launch were embarrassed when thousands of the balloons quickly came back to earth. Balloons choked highways and briefly caused Burke Lakefront Airport to shut down. So many ended up in Lake Erie that they caused a halt to the search for two missing fishermen. *(Courtesy of Michael Polly)*

off inflation at number 1,429,643—still well above the Disney record.

At 1:50 p.m., almost fifteen minutes before schedule, Jerry Jarrett, general campaign chairman for United Way, walked to a microphone. His voice boomed out across Public Square: "Are you ready, Cleveland?"

Then, the balloons were released.

Treb Heining was right. It was one of the most amazing sights I had ever seen. The balloons looked like a giant cloud rising over the square. Some balloons danced against the buildings. The mass rose slowly, almost majestically. Other people described it as a mushroom-shaped monster rising above the

Cleveland skyline. One woman told me it looked like a volcano erupted, spewing giant confetti.

Thousands and thousands of balloons filled the sky, blotting out the clouds. At first the balloons started drifting south, away from downtown. But then the storm hit, and many of the balloons changed direction and started drifting over the lakefront and began to fall back to earth, driven down by the wind and rain.

My friend and colleague Scott Sabol, meteorologist at WJW-TV, recently looked up the weather records for that day and explained what happened.

"The air was very humid and unstable," Scott said. "A warm front to the north of Cleveland dropped south. A drop like this would create a sharp wind shift to the north." He added, "Given these weather conditions, the balloons should not have been launched."

Balloons were now raining down on the Shoreway, where startled motorists driving at highway speeds began crashing into railings and even each other. Some said they were dodging the falling balloons; others admitted they were distracted by the sudden appearance of the gaily colored balloons. At one point the Shoreway looked like a rainbow-colored river of balloons.

After we got our video of the balloon launch on Public Square, we headed back to Burke Lakefront Airport to check on the search for the missing fishermen. There, so many balloons covered the runway that the airport was forced to close for take-offs and landings for half an hour while workers scooped them off the runways.

I spotted the Coast Guard helicopter that had been searching for the two fishermen. The pilot, who had just landed amidst the balloon barrage, told me that they had to call off their search because of all the descending balloons. He said, "It was like flying through an asteroid field."

Coast Guardsmen in boats later complained that their search was hampered by the sheer number of bobbing balloons in the lake, which made it almost impossible to spot a person in the water.

The Cleveland lakefront was not the only place where balloons came back to earth. Winds carried a large cluster south all the way to Medina County, more than thirty miles south of Cleveland, where they fell from the sky over a Montville horse farm owned by Louise Nowakowski, who raised Arabian show horses. The horses were spooked by all the balloons falling from the sky and bolted, running into a wire fence where one was permanently injured.

After three days of searching for the missing fishermen, the Coast Guard suspended their search. It would be days before their bodies finally washed ashore.

In 1986, the United Way announced that their drive had set a new record of pledges: more than fifty million dollars that year. However, the balloon launch as a money-raiser had not lived up to its expectations.

In the months to come, the wife of Raymond Broderick, one of the dead fishermen, sued the United Way for $3.2 million. The case was later settled for an undisclosed sum.

Horse owner Louise Nowakowski also went to court over her injured horse and sued United Way for $100,000. This lawsuit also was settled for an undisclosed amount.

Treb Heining returned to California, where he continued in the balloon business. At the time of this writing, his work has been seen in numerous Super Bowls and other big events down through the years. He created an innovative balloon-within-a-balloon for Disney: Each time you see a Mickey Mouse balloon inside another balloon, that's Heining's work.

It may have been the litigation or increased concern over the environment, but Cleveland became the last city to hold the Guinness world's record for launching the most helium-filled latex balloons released at one time. In 2015, Guinness announced that they had retired the category and no longer prints it in its books.

The *Roger Blough* Inferno

IN LORAIN, OHIO, in 1968 they laid the keel for what was at that time the largest ship ever built entirely on the Great Lakes.

This monster lake-going freighter would be as long as the ill-fated *Titanic*.

Imagine this: At 833 feet long when completed, if stood on end, this ship would be more than a hundred feet taller than Cleveland's Terminal Tower.

The ship had been ordered built by the U. S. Steel Corporation, and it was to be constructed at the Lorain Yards of the American Shipbuilding Company. With its great length and width—105 feet at its widest, the ship would be capable of transporting three times the load of steel-making materials that other lake freighters of the time could carry.

By June 1971, the ship was nearing completion. It was to be named after the former chairman of U. S. Steel Corporation, Roger Blough.

On June 5, with the band from nearby Bay Village High School playing, Mrs. Helen Blough, wife of Roger Blough, smashed a champagne bottle over the bow of the giant ship at the christening ceremony. And the owner of the American Shipbuilding Company, George Steinbrenner III, had just announced plans to invite people from Lorain and the surrounding county to visit the shipyard and tour the great ship at an open house celebration that he was planning as a "thank you" to folks in Lorain for passing a bond issue that a made it possible to build such a boat.

On Thursday, June 24, the builders were getting the ship ready for its sea trails in just a few days. The fuel tanks for the two giant diesel engines were being filled, with already about 27,000 gallons of fuel oil on board. Workmen were scattered through the ship putting the finishing touches on the construction.

According to a later report in the *Elyria Chronicle Telegram*, two men working in the engine room, Kenneth Elkin and Zoltan Zoltai, both told company investigators that about 9:30 in the morning they suddenly noticed a leak in a fuel line. Before they could do anything, they said, the leak ruptured, and fuel oil poured onto an electric light bulb, which broke and sparked a fire. The fire quickly grew, fed by the gushing fuel. Zoltai said he grabbed a fire extinguisher and emptied it on the fire, but it did little good. The fire was growing fast. He ordered everyone out of the engine room.

Just below Zoltai's and Elkin's location, in the bottom of the ship, in a cramped tunnel-like area, were several men. "We had been down here only about 20 minutes," foreman Jessie Godsey told the *Plain Dealer*. "Air was being pumped into us. Suddenly I saw a bunch of smoke and fire. I ran for some Scott Paks (portable air devices) and tried to get back to my men, but I just couldn't make it."

Godsey said he ran to a manhole that led from the area and crawled through it, only to find more smoke. Smoke was so thick he could hardly see. He made it through a grating on the floor of the engine room and through the smoke spotted a stairway leading to the upper decks. Reaching the stairway, he found a door that apparently had been closed to contain the fire. He started pounding on the door. He told reporters he didn't think he was going to get out of the burning ship until suddenly the

The fuel tanks contained 20,000 gallons of fuel. Firefighters poured thousands of gallons of water and foam into the ship, trying to extinguish the blaze. Their efforts were hampered by the extreme heat caused by the burning fuel. The decks became so hot that they melted firefighters's boots and hoses. *(Lorain Historical Society)*

door opened and he was rescued. He was taken to St. Joseph Hospital in Lorain suffering from smoke inhalation.

Meanwhile, others who had gotten out of the inside of the ship were being gathered on the top deck, and supervisors did quick head counts to see if anyone was missing. Four men did not answer the roll call: Leonard Moore, Jr., 34, of Elyria; Clyde Burdue, 60, of Vermilion; John Alexander, 28, of Lorain; and George Adams, 44, of Lorain. All had been working in the inner bottom of the ship under the engine room like Godsey and were apparently trapped there beneath the fire.

The need for a drink of water probably saved the life of another worker who had been in the bottom of the ship working. The *Lorain Journal* reported that Willie Chavis, 47, of Elyria, said he had taken a break to climb to the top deck for a cooling drink. He was just getting ready to go back down into the bowels of the ship when he saw black smoke pouring out of the stack. He knew something was wrong.

Alarms started going off, and supervisors started organizing firefighting efforts. When it was realized that four men were missing, Chavis was one of the volunteers who grabbed a ship's firehose and carried it back into the engine room.

"I was walking along the catwalk over the engine room spraying water down onto the engine," Chavis told the *Lorain Journal*. "There were really a lot of flames and smoke right then and I thought we would be able to get to them"—the men trapped below the engine room.

"All of a sudden something happened," Chavis continued. "I don't know if it was an explosion, but I really don't think so, because I didn't feel anything. But a helluva lot of smoke, real thick and heavy, came shooting up at me from the engine room floor. I was still spraying water, but I couldn't see a thing. Then, I couldn't breathe at all."

Unable to see or breathe, Chavis dropped to the grated floor and by feel crawled his way to a nearby doorway, where he passed out. He was found there by other rescuers, who rushed him to the hospital.

When the first units of the Lorain Fire Department arrived, they immediately called for backup. The department had little experience in fighting shipboard fires of this magnitude.

"I was just a young firefighter," now-retired fire lieutenant Al Baldie recalls. "I had never been trained for combatting a fire in a ship this large." He and two other firefighters were lifted on a pallet by a gantry crane onto the deck of the burning ship. From there, they went down into the hold at about the middle of the vessel. "We made our way to the rear, where the engine room was located. The entire steel wall that separated the engine room from the hold was cherry red with heat. We realized we could not get through that way and had to go back topside."

Firefighter Tony Volak was at the time a ten-year veteran of the department. He recalls, "When we got there it was going pretty good. We tried to fight the flames in the space above the engine room. We went in several times, but the flames would die down and then roll up from the floor and cover the ceiling. When that happened, our officers pulled us back out until we could try it again. We must have gone in that room three or four times without making any headway."

Soon, the entire fire department was on scene with all of their equipment.

Fire chief Henry Pierce took personal command. As reported later in the *Plain Dealer*, he ordered shipyard welders to burn a three-foot hole in the steel side of the burning ship about where shipyard personnel thought the four missing men might be. When it was done, firefighters tried to enter the ship through the hole to search for the missing workers, but the smoke and fire was too intense and drove them back out of the burning vessel.

There were explosions in the engine room. Firefighters and shipyard workers tried to spread foam on the flames, but with the ruptured fuel line feeding the fire they soon used up all of their foam-making material. Calls went out to Cleveland Hopkins Airport and other fire departments for more foam and equipment.

I was working as a reporter at WJW-TV in Cleveland at the time and was assigned to take a camera crew and get to Lorain as quickly as possible.

When videographers Cook Goodwin and Peter Miller, and I arrived at the Lorain Shipyards, police and security guards had blocked off all shipyard entrances on Colorado Avenue. I managed to convince one of the security guards to contact

Marsh Samuel, who handled media relations for Steinbrenner, the Lorain Shipyards, and American Shipbuilding. Samuel ordered the guards to let us through and met us at the executive offices that overlooked the shipyards and the burning ship.

I told Goodwin and Miller to split up and start shooting video while I went into the headquarters to be briefed by Samuel. While there, I needed to find a telephone so I could call in a report to the news desk back at the station as well as WJW Radio.

After getting the basic facts of what had happened, I asked Samuel to use a phone. He pointed me to an office next to the reception area where we were standing. I was just finishing my call when I could hear the front door to the office slam open and a very angry George Steinbrenner III shouting at Marsh Samuel.

Steinbrenner, who had not been at the shipyards when the fire started and had just arrived, was not happy to see TV camera operators and other photographers on his property. He was almost screaming at the soft-spoken Marsh Samuel, who was trying to convince him that in a major story like this, it was good to cooperate with the news media.

Pretending I had not heard the loud discussion, I walked out of the office, introduced myself to a visibly surprised Steinbrenner, and started asking him about the missing men. It was like a switch had been thrown. Steinbrenner went from angry to the calm, caring corporate executive.

"There are four men unaccounted for," Steinbrenner told me. "The only thing important is the lives of those four men."

And with that, he left the office to meet with yard and fire officials to get briefed on the latest efforts to knock down the fire and, hopefully, rescue the men.

By now, hours had gone by since the start of the fire, yet thick black smoke still poured from the stack. Several holes had been

During the fire a total of eighteen firefighters and shipyard workers were taken to area hospitals, mostly with smoke inhalation. *(Cleveland Public Library)*

made in the sides of the ship in an effort to find the missing workers.

The fire department had a tugboat with high-pressure water cannons, but it could not get close enough to the *Blough* because the drydock where the ship was burning was almost a thousand feet from the Black River.

Firefighters kept running low on foam-making material. A chartered airplane brought more from Detroit, landing at Long Airport on Route 58, where pickup trucks were waiting to carry the material to the shipyards. Fire departments from as far away as Cleveland suburbs Shaker Heights and Fairview Park sent foam-making equipment. The Cleveland Fire Department offered their equipment for fighting airplane fires plus ten fire-proof suits.

But still the fire continued to burn. Firefighter Al Baldie recalls that the steel ship was like a giant "Potbelly stove"—the decks so hot that their boots and shoes were melting into the surface.

Even hundreds of feet away from the giant ship, we reporters and camera operators could feel the heat and hear sounds of the warping steel plates.

The Lorain Fire Department Snorkel Unit, which was spraying foam and water down onto the ship, also was affected by the heat. Baldie said they had to get sheets of asbestos to place on the floor of the platform to try to protect their hoses and equipment.

A steady stream of ambulances seemed to be going in and out of the shipyards during that long afternoon and evening. A total of eighteen firefighters, shipyard officials, and workers were taken to the local hospital with smoke inhalation and other injuries.

About 7 p.m. the main fuel tank, containing about 20,000 gallons of fuel, was ruptured by the extreme heat and exploded, causing more problems for the already exhausted firefighters and volunteers.

Lorain fire chief Henry Pierce, quoted in the *Plain Dealer*, said "[The] fuel in the tank is burning like a huge cauldron."

Shortly after the explosion, five firefighters, led by Patrick Costello, put on the fire-resistant suits and entered the flame- and heat-filled engine room to try to put an extension on a foam-making machine that would allow them to pour foam directly into the burning tank.

"I'm not going to be happy until I see white smoke coming from the ship's stack," Fire Chief Pierce said.

It was well after midnight, more than fifteen hours since the fire had begun, when the combined efforts of a hundred firefighters from several departments plus shipyard volunteers

This aerial photo was taken late in the day. White smoke indicates that the firefighters had finally controlled the burning oil in the engine room, but it would be well into the next day before the fires were finally extinguished.
(Cleveland Public Library)

were able to bring the blaze under control and finally extinguish the fire.

But the search for the missing men was still held. Thousands of gallons of water had been poured into the ship, and the temperature inside was still like a giant oven. Rescue workers had to wait for the ship to cool down and for pumps to start emptying the water and residue from the firefighting foam.

It would be Friday evening before firefighters were finally

able to make their way under the floor of the engine room to the lowest portion of the ship where the men had been working.

The first grim discovery was the body of Clyde Burdue. Then, about ten minutes later, searchers found the remains of John Alexander. It took another twenty minutes to find the bodies of Leonard Moore and George Adams. All four men had not been burned but had died from a lack of oxygen.

George Steinbrenner personally broke the news to the men's families, who had been keeping a vigil in the company offices. A few minutes later Steinbrenner held a news conference. He appeared with tears in his eyes, and in an emotion-filled voice told reporters, "We did a fantastic job against terrific odds, but the men are dead."

Afterward . . .

Damage to the *Roger Blough* was estimated at $10 million (equivalent to $70 million dollars in 2022).

The ship was rebuilt. It finally set sail on its maiden voyage in June 1972.

In 1973, George Steinbrenner led a group that purchased the New York Yankees. He went on to have a tumultuous career as a baseball team owner.

On November 11, 1975, the *Roger Blough* took part in the search for the missing lake freighter *The Edmund Fitzgerald* in Lake Superior. The Blough found and recovered an empty 25-person life raft from the ill-fated ship.

A decline in lake shipping caused American Shipbuilding Company to close several of its Great Lakes locations, and its Lorain Shipyards went out of business in 1983. The shipyards were converted to a riverfront housing development called Harborwalk.

As of this writing, the *Roger Blough* continues to sail the Great Lakes, nearly a half-century after the disastrous fire. The ship has had several owners over the years.

In January 2021, the *Roger Blough* was in drydock near Green Bay, Wisconsin, when it caught fire and sustained much damage. According to a report on WBAY-TV in Sturgeon Bay, Wisconsin, like the fire fifty years before, the blaze was centered in the engine room, and it required dozens of firefighters working for hours to finally extinguish the flames. The ship was in drydock and only a single man, the shipkeeper, was on board, and he escaped uninjured. As of this writing, the cause of the 2021 fire has not been determined. Because of the heavy damage, which firefighters estimated at $20 million, there is speculation that the *Roger Blough* may have sailed its final journey.

The Who Concert
Stampede in Cincinnati

WHEN A CROWD gets out of control, it can get dangerous quickly.

I learned that firsthand in September 1964 when, as a young reporter, I attempted to cover the arrival of the Beatles for their first appearance in Ohio. Thousands of teenagers, mostly girls, had invaded Cleveland Hopkins Airport at midnight, all hoping to see the four young musicians as they left their airplane.

In those days, when security concerns were few, the airport had a public observation deck where you could watch planes arrive and depart. It was located off an upper lobby where you could walk out over the area where passengers got off and on the planes. That evening, as more than two thousand teens descended on the airport, so many young people crowded the deck that police tried to close it.

Then, when youngsters started climbing down the side of the building to the actual airfield, visions of propellers chopping up young people caused police to reroute the airplane carrying the Beatles to the tank factory (which later became the I-X Center) at the other end of the airfield.

Fifteen minutes after the Beatles had landed and were on their way to their hotel (under police escort), police at the airport announced over the public address system that the

Beatles had already landed and were now gone. It caused an immediate uproar.

The youngsters, like some huge tidal wave, tried to leave the observation deck at one time. There was screaming and crying; chairs were overturned and plants knocked over, and suddenly I found myself and other reporters I was standing next to being propelled by this mass of humanity off the observation deck and toward the airport lobby, where two glass doors led into the larger room and the exit. As the crowd pressed me closer and closer to the glass, it became hard to breathe. I suddenly realized that if I lost my footing and fell, I really might be trampled to death. I was using my arms to push away the upset mob and prepared myself for the worst as we approached the closed glass doors. I thought the doors might smash, causing many injuries, but fortunately they opened and the crowd flowed through, eventually dissipating in the larger lobby.

I still remember the jolt of fear I felt when I realized I could not move and had to literally let the crowd carry me along to avoid being trampled.

That evening came back to me on December 3, 1979. I was working in the WJW-TV newsroom when the first bulletin came in about a tragedy in Cincinnati.

The Who, a popular British rock band made up at that time of Roger Daltrey, Pete Townshend, Kenney Jones, and John Entwistle, were on the U.S. leg of a world tour. They were slated to play just one concert at Riverfront Coliseum (later renamed Heritage Bank Center) on the banks of the Ohio River in downtown Cincinnati.

Fans were excited, and the coliseum sold out weeks before the concert. Of the more than 18,000 seats, the majority of the tickets were ten dollars for general admission, or "festival seating"—meaning there were no seat assignments; first come, first served.

Mike Simkin was one of the lucky ones to get tickets. "Once we had those tickets, it was like gold," he recalls. "I felt like putting [them] in a safe deposit box. The anticipation was amazing."

The morning of the show, many of the young fans began to gather early at the coliseum.

"Back in those days we'd camp," Mike Wergers, one of the concertgoers, told WCPO-TV in Cincinnati years later. "We got there at noon on show day to get ready to go for the concert that was later in the day."

Mike Simkin was there early, too. He recalls that he and his best friend, Stephen Preston, were joined by three other friends from Finneytown. Doors were supposed to open at 7 p.m. By 5 p.m., a crowd estimated at about 7,000 had gathered, and people were amassing around the entrance doors to the coliseum.

Mike Simkin said that he and his friends were about fifteen feet from a door when the crowd first started pressing in toward them and, as he recalls, "sort of started swaying. You couldn't stand in one place. You were kind of at the mercy of the crowd." Simkin had been in crowds before, but this time it was different. "Some knuckleheads were running from the rear and throwing themselves at the crowd at the door. Things were getting a little crazy." In a matter of moments, amid the pushing and shoving, he was separated from his friends. Then, he realized that just breathing was a problem. "It was like a boa constrictor crushing you. I managed to get my arms down, and it became a matter of survival. I had to use my arms to try to force other bodies away just so I could breathe."

By 7 p.m. the situation was becoming ominous. Fans had assumed that all entrance doors would all open at once, at 7 p.m., about an hour before the concert was to start. They did not. By 7:20 p.m., anxious fans pounded on entrance doors. One pair of doors at the southwest corner of the plaza had been forced open, but the rest remained closed.

Then, the sound system inside the arena came to life. It was playing a movie trailer about the Who, but fans who heard the music mistakenly believed the concert was starting. Now, they joined a mass of other people who were surging toward the only open door.

Chaos erupted.

There was pushing and screaming. Bottles were being broken. So many people tried to get through the doorways at once that the entrances became blocked by bodies.

"I think that my boyfriend walked right over top of me and didn't know it," Diana Culbert later told the *Cincinnati Enquirer*. She was at the bottom of a pile of bodies trying to get through the door. "I laid there. They were laying on me and standing on my leg. You could feel their feet move back and forth on your leg. I wanted out so bad, but I couldn't move. I was pinned down on the ground." Finally, with a free arm she grabbed the arms of two men inside the door who were able to yank her out of the pile of people. Her shoes and socks were gone and her coat and jeans were in tatters. She was taken to the hospital for treatment of leg injuries.

Her boyfriend, Marty Stonely, also talked with reporters. "It was disgusting," he said. "Whoever was the strongest stayed up. I went down about five times. You would grab onto somebody and pull yourself up. It was like five thousand pounds against you. I was just praying. I didn't think I was going to get out alive. It was frightening."

David Hack told the *New York Times* that he and his wife, Karen, had a similar experience. "'For a while it was the usual,' he said, 'until they opened that door. It started getting crowded, and crowded and crowded and nobody let up. A few times you're up in midair and getting turned around backwards.' He said he was very concerned for Karen, who was pregnant. 'All I could do is keep both arms around my wife and just fight people off trying to make sure she didn't get an elbow in the gut. It was the only thing I could do. Then my wife, after a while, said she was standing on someone and I tried to let her back. And let people get back. We got away and the guy was on the ground and wouldn't get up. We got pushed away and couldn't help him. People just ended up walking back over him.'"

Mike Simkin, who was in the middle of the crowd, remembers, "It was about this time they started passing people to the rear. I remember four or five limp bodies that were handed right over our heads to the rear of the crowd. I don't know if they were dead or alive."

Mark Williams, 20, told the *Cincinnati Enquirer* that he was trapped inside the panicking mob for about forty minutes. He said people lying on the concrete were "begging for their lives." He said, "I was all the way on the bottom of the cement. People on the bottom were yelling they were dying. I grabbed this guy by the shirt and said, 'Wake up.' I slapped him in the face. He did not move."

Barbara Streff, 29, and her husband, Michael, were separated from each other by the crowd. When she reached the turnstile, the only security officer in sight began shouting at the crowd to back up. "I tried to back up but most of the people kept pushing," Streff told the *Cincinnati Enquirer*. Finally, she and Michael reached each other and tried to retreat. "We could see bodies, at least four of them, on the floor. They had their shirts off and were giving them mouth-to-mouth resuscitation to try to revive them."

The Streffs, who had reserved-seat tickets for the concert, decided to go home. "Some kids came running by with this person in their arms. We saw another one on a table. They had his shirt off trying to bring him around," Barbara said. She also said that many police officers they encountered on the plaza outside the coliseum were not aware of the fatalities.

Jim Camden, 16, told the *Cincinnati Enquirer* that he and a friend were next to each other in line when the rush began. "It was crazy, it happens all the time. You just don't want to get in front of a line at a concert." He said his friend fell to the cement and was trampled by others anxious to get into the concert. "He was just lying on the ground. No one did anything. No one cared."

Suzanne Sudrack, 15, told the *Plain Dealer*, "You could see people getting hurt. People were flailing elbows and smashing noses. You could see people going down."

Ray Schwertman, 49, an usher at the coliseum, told the *Plain Dealer* that the crowd surged through a door just before the gates were to open at 7 p.m. "First they threw a bottle through a window in the door. Then they pushed through the hole, making it bigger. Three or four of us tried to hold them back, but it was no use. They carried in one boy and laid him on a table and he died. Others were laying out on the plaza."

Jeff Chaney, a concertgoer who was also an army veteran, tried to help by pulling some of the victims from a pile near the entrance. The *Columbus Dispatch* reported him saying, "I really couldn't believe it. I've never seen anything like it, even in the army, and I never want to see anything like it again."

Chaney said one girl was still alive and clutching his leg as he tried to unsort the pile of people, but by the time the girl was freed, she was dead. "People just didn't seem to care. They could see the people all piled up, and they still tried to climb over them just to get up front."

Mike Simkin said that when caught in the mob at the open door, he could see what appeared to be police officers standing inside the coliseum in front of the glass doors that were still locked. "Whoever made the decision not to open those doors and relieve the pressure—well, all I can say is they have blood on their hands," he said.

When another of the glass doors opened, Simkin and about thirty other people lunged for the opening. "I managed to grab the steel bar that supports the door, and I used all my strength to propel myself through that door," he said. "I literally tumbled inside the coliseum. I was wet with sweat. It was 20 degrees outside. Looking back I could see a cloud of fog created by the breath of so many people trying to get through the doorway."

Benjamin Bowes told the *Cincinnati Enquirer* that he got inside and watched the entire concert not knowing that his brother, Peter, 18 years old, had been killed in the melee at the door. Bowes did not learn of the tragedy until later that evening when he returned home. He said, "I was at the same doors but didn't know it. Peter was with his friends and I was with another group. There was a lot of pushing, it was the scariest thing I have ever been through."

As firefighters, rescue workers, and police began to arrive, the plaza outside the coliseum resembled a war zone. Abandoned shoes, broken bottles, and items of clothing were everywhere.

It was a surreal scene. Ambulances and police cars lined the street, lights flashing, as many fans were just arriving, totally unaware of what was happening at one of the entrances.

Despite the pandemonium on the plaza, thousands of people did make it inside the coliseum, and the concert began about 8:20 p.m. *Rolling Stone* magazine reported later that the members of the Who had not been told of the unfolding tragedy just outside the building. Cincinnati safety director Richard Castellini later told the *Cincinnati Enquirer* that he considered stopping the concert but decided against it when he discovered the problem was outside the building and not inside, where the concert was going on. In fact, many people said afterwards that they had enjoyed the concert and had no idea of the tragedy until they were on the way home and heard about it on the radio.

Jeff Hirsh saw bulletins about the tragedy on local TV. A

reporter himself, he was just starting a new job for WLW-TV and had only been in Cincinnati for two weeks—and did not yet have a telephone. He had to go to a neighbor and ask to use his phone to call the TV station and ask if they wanted him to come to work. They did. He was assigned to cover events at police headquarters, and he hurried there.

"Police stations are not usually a center of chaos," Hirsch recalls. "It's been forty years, but I still remember the phones were ringing, people were coming in, looking for their kids. The media was trying to get information. The feeling I got was this just doesn't happen in Cincinnati."

The dead and the injured had been taken to hospitals all over the city. Hospitals like General, Mercy, Deaconess, Good Samaritan, and Christ all reported they received patients from the Riverfront Coliseum.

It took a couple of hours before city officials got the count: eleven people dead and at least twenty-six injured. It was a very sad night for the Queen City.

Dr. Frank P. Cleveland, the Hamilton County coroner, told the *Cincinnati Enquirer* that the eleven people killed in the stampede "died from asphyxiation and most had (other) minor injuries." Cleveland said asphyxiation was a result of the victim's body being compressed by the weight of the others that were piled on top of them.

Mike Simkin, once inside the coliseum, went to the floor near the sound board where he met up with his Finneytown friends. Nineteen-year-old Steve Preston was not there. "We weren't concerned," Mike says. "We thought he may have met up with another friend and was somewhere in the crowd." It was only after the concert, when they had returned to where they parked their car and Preston did not show up, that they began to get concerned.

Simkin says that when he and his friends got home that night,

Reports on the tragedy covered the
entire front page of the next day's
Cincinnati Post.

they checked with Stephan Preston's parents, who told them
Steve had not returned home from the concert. Now fearing the
worst, Mike and some friends returned to the coliseum. They
did not find Steve but heard that some unidentified bodies were
at General Hospital, so they went there next. There, they were
directed to the morgue. They described Stephan to a nurse, who
went into another room and came back with his jacket. All three
of them sank to the floor as they realized their friend was among
the casualties.

Dan Burns was looking for his wife, 18-year-old Connie Burns,
a mother of two—a 3-year-old daughter and a 5-month-old son.
The *Dayton Daily News* reported that they had been part of a

group of thirty-five young adults from the Dayton-Middletown area travelling by charter bus to the concert. Connie and Dan apparently were separated in the crowd fighting to get through the door. He began searching for her all through the crowd on the plaza, then finally went back to the bus. She was not there. He eventually contacted the police, and they took Dan to the morgue to see if his wife was among bodies brought there. Two hours later he came back in tears. His wife was dead.

The Associated Press reported that two more of the dead came from Finneytown, a small community on the north side of Cincinnati: 15-year-old Karen Morrison and 15-year-old Jacquiline Eckerle. Also killed in the crush were: Teva Ladd, 24, from Newtown; David Joseph Heck, 19 of Highland Heights, Kentucky; James Warmoth, 21, of Franklin Township; Bryan Wagner, 17, Fort Thomas, Kentucky; Walter Adams, Jr., 22 from Trotwood, Ohio; and Phillip Kent Snyder, 20, of Warren County.

It was only after the Who had played their final encore that their manager took them aside and told them about the number of deaths and injuries that had occurred outside the Riverfront Coliseum. According to *Rolling Stone* Magazine, band members were devastated by the news.

The Who left Cincinnati that night for the next stop of their tour: Buffalo, New York, scheduled for the next night. The *Buffalo News* reported that Tuesday night Roger Daltrey opened the show by addressing the audience. "I'd just like to say, you all know what happened yesterday," Daltrey said. "There is nothing we can do. We feel totally shattered. But life goes on. We lost a lot of family yesterday. And this show is for them." The audience gave them a standing ovation.

In Cincinnati there was a lot of finger-pointing, but no charges were ever brought against anybody involved in the concert.

Dozens of lawsuits were filed—against Riverfront Coliseum and its directors and president, against the City of Cincinnati,

Three of the people killed that night were Finneytown graduates or attendees. Members of the school community started a memorial foundation to keep their memory alive by raising funds for a scholarship in their names. From left to right, Stephan Preston (class of '79), Jackie Eckerle (class of '82) and Karen Morrison (class of '82). *(Courtesy of the P.E.M. Memorial Committee)*

the concert promoter, and the Who. All the cases were settled out of court after dragging through the legal system for nearly five years.

The unbelievable pain suffered by the families was explained to the Associated Press by Mary and Richard Bowes, parents of 18-year-old Peter Bowes, who was killed in the crush at the concert. They had opted out of a class-action lawsuit filed by other families who lost a loved one in the concert tragedy and instead sued the same organizations for $8.5 million in compensatory and punitive damages. It looked like their case was finally going to be heard after five years of legal wrangling when they also agreed to settle out of court. Richard Bowes explained their decision. "We wanted it all to come out, but we didn't have the resources—financial or mental—to continue," he told Associated Press. "So we settled. It was getting hard on the family. After all, it was hard to begin with."

The Boweses also said the legal process resulted in lawyers digging into their personal lives. They said a son was questioned for thirteen hours. Mary Bowes compared the case to a rape investigation. "The victims turned out to be on trial," she said. "We had to prove that our whole family wasn't guilty." They also said that no matter how the trial ended, it would have been appealed and then dragged on even longer.

It was generally agreed that the festival seating—general admission with unassigned seats—was a major factor in the tragedy. Just days after the concert, Cincinnati City Council passed an ordinance banning the sale of general admission tickets at any large gathering in the city.

Life went on.

The city lifted its ban on general admission tickets after twenty-five years, reportedly over concern that major touring acts were skipping Cincinnati. Survivor Mike Simpkin, says that after city council lifted the ban, "We in Finneytown and the families of the deceased and all who still carried wounds from the tragedy were not happy at all, as you can imagine. It felt like a slap in the face to us."

There were efforts to keep the memory alive of the concert victims.

In 2009, two Finneytown High School alumni, John Hutchins and Steve Bentz, class of 1980, proposed that a stone memorial bench be placed in front of the Performing Arts Center at Finneytown High School to honor the memory of the three Finneytown students killed at the concert: Stephan Preston, Jacquiline Eckerle, and Karen Morrison. The idea became reality in 2010, and it began to grow. A committee had been formed with Hutchins and Bentz, joined by Sandra and Walt Medlock, Toni Hutchins, and Fred Wittenbaum. They created a living memorial by establishing the P.E.M. Memorial Scholarship Fund for students at Finneytown High School who are pursuing a career

Roger Daltrey, lead singer of the Who, poses with members of the P.E.M. Memorial Committee of Finneytown High School on July 2, 2018. It was the first time that any member of the band had been back to Cincinnati since the tragedy. Standing, *left to right*, are Steve-O Bentz, Fred Wittenbaum, Walt Medlock, and Brad Rubin. Seated on the bench are Roger Daltrey, Toni Hutchins, and John Hutchins. *(Courtesy of the P.E.M. Memorial Committee)*

in the musical arts. By 2021, the fund had raised and granted over a hundred thousand dollars in scholarships at the school. The memorial bench was surrounded by a brick plaza, and in the school an exhibit honors the three students who died, along with plaques with their names and pictures inscribed.

On December 3, 2015, a bronze plaque listing the names of all the dead and telling about the tragic event was placed in front of the coliseum.

The Who continued their long and successful career, and in 1990 were inducted into the Rock and Roll Hall of Fame, but as of this writing never performed another concert in Cincinnati.

In 2017, P.E.M. Memorial committee member Fred Wittenbaum had an idea. He had been communicating with members of the Who, had spoken with Roger Daltrey several times, and had even been invited backstage when the band played in Kentucky in 2013. Because of this connection, the band had made contributions to the P.E.M. memorial over a period of time. So when Wittenbaum learned that Roger Daltrey was going to be doing a solo performance near Dayton, he launched a flurry of emails trying to get Daltrey to include Finneytown in his Ohio visit. It worked. On July 2, 2018, Roger Daltrey's personal jet landed at a small airport near Miamisburg, and Fred Wittenbaum was there to meet him and drove him to Finneytown.

By mutual agreement between Daltrey and the P.E.M. committee, the media was not told of Daltrey's visit. Daltrey had asked to meet with family members of the three Finneytown young adults who had lost their lives at the concert. This was arranged, and it was an emotional meeting as evidenced on a home video shot by Wittenbaum's then-16-year-old son, Jeremy. "They were so young," Daltrey says as he gazes at the memorial exhibit. He goes on to tell the assembled group that he had always felt the band should have cancelled the Buffalo concert and stayed to "mourn with the families." Daltrey was at the school for an hour or more, signing autographs, posing for pictures, and chatting with the families.

In 2019, during an interview on WCPO-TV marking the fortieth anniversary of the tragedy, the Who announced they were coming back to the Cincinnati area and that some of the proceeds would go to the P.E.M. scholarship fund. The event was slated for April 23, 2020. Unfortunately, the concert was cancelled due to a worldwide pandemic.

As of this writing, Fred Wittenbaum is very determined and optimistic that the concert will be rescheduled. The Who, he says, will come back to Cincinnati.

The Zanesville Exotic Animal Escape

IT STARTED IN the northeast corner of Sam Kopchak's pasture. Sam, a retired seventh grade science teacher, had recently fulfilled one of his retirement dreams: to own a horse. He shared a home with his mother, Dolores, on Kopchak Road, and he had just days before purchased a Pinto named Red. Today, October 11, 2011, was the first day he had let Red run free in the small pasture behind the barn. It was about 4:30 p.m. when Sam came into the pasture to put the horse in the barn for the night.

The horse was acting very nervous and running away from him. So Sam took a bucket of water and walked up to the corner of his property where the horse took a drink and allowed him to put a lead rope on his halter.

That is when Sam happened to look across the boundary fence into Terry Thompson's adjoining pasture and saw a herd of Thompson's horses running frantically in circles.

"That's just not normal for horses," Kopchak recalls. Then, he saw a dark figure near the horses. It took Kopchak a second or so to realize what the dark figure was. A bear. The bear had apparently been stalking the horses. Then it took off running toward the interstate highway, away from Sam and Red.

Realizing that it was the bear that had spooked the animals, he started leading Red back to the barn. Kopchak was not too surprised. He knew that Terry Thompson, his next-door neighbor, had a collection of exotic animals, including bears. But as Kopchak continued leading Red back to the barn, he became more concerned.

"As I was walking, I felt like something was looking at me," he says. "I turned, and right beside the fence was a huge full-grown male African lion. He was about thirty feet away on the other side of a four-foot-tall wire fence."

Luckily, the wind was blowing in the right direction, and the horse did not pick up the scent of the lion. Kopchak said he had read somewhere that you should never look a lion in the eye. So he walked a bit faster, not daring to look back over his shoulder.

"We finally reached the barn. That was the longest walk of my life."

Kopchak quickly closed the barn doors, and because his cell phone service was poor, he called his mother, Dolores, known to most folks as Dolly, who lived in the family home at the end of the driveway. He asked her to use her more reliable landline and call the sheriff to report that a bear and a lion were loose.

But Mrs. Kopchak did not call the sheriff. This sort of thing— animals getting loose—had happened before, so she instead did the neighborly thing and dialed her neighbor, Terry Thompson, to alert him that some of his animals appeared to be loose. Thompson did not answer, though, so then she dialed the sheriff's office.

In the basement of the Muskingum County Jail in downtown Zanesville, it was about 5 p.m. when a dispatcher took the call.

"This is Mrs. Kopchak. On Kopchak Road. We live next to Terry Thompson, and there is a bear and a lion out."

This calm, matter-of-fact call coming in on the emergency 9-1-1 line was not unusual. Terry Thompson was well known to the county sheriff's department, which had responded to dozens of such calls over the years regarding the sprawling 74-acre farm that bordered Interstate 70 just west of town.

Thompson, a Vietnam War veteran, along his wife, Marian, a retired local schoolteacher, had gathered a large collection of exotic animals: Bengal tigers, African lions, bears, and other large predatory animals as well as some horses and other livestock. Over the years, there had been complaints to the Muskingum County Sheriff's office of animal mistreatment, and it was not the first time some of his animals had gotten loose.

Back at the barn behind the Kopchak home, Sam was still looking out the window at the activity in his neighbor's field. The number of animals was growing. The bear and the lion had now been joined by a larger bear, and then another lion started loping across the field. They were soon joined by a wolf. And then Sam spotted an even bigger predator: a fully grown Bengal tiger. It was like Noah's Ark had just emptied out in central Ohio.

Muskingum County sheriff Matt Lutz recalls that one of the first of his deputies to reach the scene was Deputy Jonathon Merry, who had been in his patrol car in nearby Zanesville when he got the call that a bear and a lion were running loose at the Thompson Farm.

Merry pulled into the Kopchak driveway only a few minutes after receiving the call. From there he could see the Thompson property and observe what appeared to be several large animals running through the fields. He thought he saw the Bengal tiger, lions, and a couple of bears. Merry was about to knock on Dolly Kopchak's door when something caught his eye. Running down the road he had just driven on was a large gray wolf. Merry ran back to his cruiser and radioed in what he had seen and the fact that he was now pursuing a wolf. The wolf was getting close to a home. So Merry stopped the car and ran to the rear of the cruiser where he opened the trunk and got his rifle. His radio crackled. It was his superior officer instructing him to put the animal down rather than let it continue to be a threat to residents in the homes. Deputy Merry was about 250 feet away. He fired one shot, and the wolf went down.

The order to shoot had come from Muskingum County sheriff Matthew Lutz. The sheriff had been at home having dinner in nearby Philo when he was notified of the animals running loose. When he received reports from deputies who had seen more of the animals running freely, he issued the shoot-to-kill order.

"Everyone says it had to be a hard decision but it really wasn't for me," Lutz told the Pittsburgh *Post Gazette*. "I knew from being there what kind of animals he had and I knew what those animals could do."

As Deputy Merry was making sure the wolf he had just shot was dead, he heard over the police band that other deputies were facing a lion near the entrance to the Thompson property. As reported later in various sources, Merry realized that the other deputies were probably armed only with their .40 caliber handguns and perhaps a shotgun. As far as he knew, he was the only officer armed with a high-powered rifle, which would be much better suited to dealing with these big animals. So he jumped back into his patrol car and sped up the hill to the entrance of the Thompson farm. As he approached, he saw other deputies running back and forth across the driveway. He slammed on the brakes and started to get out of the car to see what was going on. He opened the door and grabbed his rifle, but when the rifle sling became entangled with the computer in the console, he left the rifle and jumped out—only to realize he had made a big mistake.

There, facing him, was a 350-pound black bear. And before Merry could react, the bear started to charge him. Merry's only weapon now was his .40 caliber handgun. He pulled it from his holster and managed to get off one shot. The charging bear

Signs were posted on Interstate 70 to warn drivers of the dangerous animals loose in the area around Zanesville on October 19, 2011.
(Reuters / Alamy Stock Photo)

sagged to the ground, mortally wounded. He was just seven feet away.

It wasn't long before news media caught on to the breaking story. Local media arrived on the scene almost immediately. Dave Nethers, a reporter for WJW-TV in Cleveland (and long-time friend and former colleague of mine), arrived to cover the story in early evening.

"It was one of those rainy, gloomy, cold Ohio days, where you don't know whether to put on a raincoat or something warm," he recalls. He said there was a feeling in the air that it was still a dangerous situation. "The sense you got was this whole Jurassic Park thing. You know, these dangerous creatures are out there, and I'm scanning the brush and every bush along the road, wondering what might be ready to jump out at you."

The situation he found was chaotic. The sheriff and his men

still had no idea just how many animals had escaped. Phone calls to the Thompson residence were going unanswered. Nearby were homes, a school soccer game in progress, and busy Interstate 70. And night was approaching.

The sheriff's staff was gathering what information they did have on Thompson. He was sixty-two years old and had been born and raised in the Zanesville area. He and his wife, both fairly well known in the area, had been high-school sweethearts. Of concern were these facts: Terry Thompson had just been released from prison after serving a year on illegal gun charges. There were reports that he and his wife had separated and that he was not only in debt but, according to his parole officer, deeply depressed over the condition of his farm.

According to Sheriff Lutz, Sergeant Steve Blake of the sheriff's department was the first officer to arrive at the entrance to the Thompson Farm. Seeing so many animals loose, he became concerned that something might have happened to Thompson. He drove up the long driveway to the house, and as he neared the building, he noticed that many cages were empty and appeared to have been forced open—wire cages had holes in them, and locks on barred doors had been cut off. Many of the big cats were roaming loose. He pulled in front of the house and sounded his car's horn. No one came out. He was alone. It would be too dangerous for him to leave the car with so many big animals on the loose, so he drove back down the driveway, where he found his boss, Sheriff Lutz, who had just arrived along with the patrol division commander, Captain Jeff LeCocq.

The two had been talking with John Moore, who lived nearby. A college student, Moore had been working at the farm six days a week taking care of the animals while Thompson was in prison. He said Marian Thompson had moved out of the farm back in the spring but continued to send him checks to pay for the animals' care. Moore had received a phone call about the loose animals, and he had come to help.

The sheriff told Moore to compile an inventory of the animals while he sent Sergeant Blake to make another attempt to enter the Thompson home in search of Terry. Blake drove back to the house; with no animals nearby, he went inside. He found only two monkeys and a dog in cages. No sign of Terry Thompson.

Blake got back into the car and was driving back to the entrance when he spotted a large tiger on top of something on the ground near one of the barns. As he got closer, Blake could see it was a white tiger, and it was feeding on a human body. Blake radioed the sheriff that he had found a body.

The response to the crisis was widening. The Ohio State Highway Patrol placed portable electric signs on Interstate 70 that displayed the message "Caution, Exotic Animals." Troopers were out in force—to look for animals that might try to cross the highway and to keep curious motorists moving along. The Columbus Zoo, on hearing the news, dispatched its capture and recovery team, armed with tranquilizer guns as well as regular weapons, to assist local law enforcement.

Back in Zanesville, the situation was still out of control. Sheriff Lutz learned from John Moore that he and his fiancé, who often helped him feed the animals, had been caring for a total of fifty-six cats, bears, and primates. But still, no one knew just how many of them were loose.

His deputies could now see multiple big cats surrounding what appeared to be a human body, but with so many of the big animals running loose, it was too dangerous for them to get close enough to determine if the person was alive or dead. The only safe way to reach the body would be to put down the animals that were near it.

Sheriff Lutz and his deputies decided first to send several armed deputies in a pickup truck to try to retrieve the body.

Deputy Todd Kanavel had just arrived driving his personal vehicle, a large pickup truck. Sergeant Blake commandeered the truck and got behind the wheel. Four deputies jumped into the bed of the truck behind him: Deputy Tony Angelo, sniper on the SWAT team; Deputy Ryan Paisley with a submachine gun; and Kanavel and Deputy Jay Lawhorne with assault rifles.

They drove slowly up the driveway and then between some cages and a barn. Suddenly, two tigers came running out of the barn straight for the truck. "They kind of took us by surprise," one of the deputies later told *GQ Magazine*. The tigers were only ten or twelve feet away when the deputies opened fire, putting them down.

They drove on until they were close enough to the body to clearly see that it was a man, lying on his back, with a large head wound. Nearby were a pistol and a pair of bolt cutters. The man was obviously dead.

They were able to check the body. It was Terry Thompson. Sheriff Lutz said that it appeared that Thompson had placed a gun barrel in his mouth and pulled the trigger. The pistol lying nearby was .357 Magnum. The sheriff also said there was a large bite mark, presumably from the tiger, on Thompson's head, and that other parts of his body had been "bothered" by the animals. Deputy Kanavel, a member of the sharpshooter group, later told *GQ* that the body appeared to have been dragged and "chewed on."

It was now dark, and rain had begun to fall.

When the Columbus Zoo team arrived, local authorities told them there were too many loose animals to try to use tranquilizer guns. Especially in the dark.

Under the best of conditions, using a tranquilizer on a dangerous animal can be tricky. Even if the dart hits the right area, it can take several minutes for the drug to take effect.

The Ohio State Patrol was heavily patrolling a seven-mile

stretch of Interstate 70, especially the part running past the Thompson Farm, using night-vision equipment to scan the roadside and weeds for the escaping animals.

Sam Kopchak in his barn had pretty much been forgotten in all the excitement. He could hear most of the shooting that was going on, and eventually he decided that the safest place for him was in his home. So, after checking on his horse, now safely in its stall, he walked quickly to his house. There, he said, he could hear shooting continue for several hours.

Throughout the night, deputies and other law enforcement officials continued to hunt down the escaped animals. They tried to use a tranquilizer gun on one tiger they found in a group of trees, but it didn't work and made the tiger more aggressive. When it tried to attack them, they had to shoot it.

"People were genuinely afraid," reporter Dave Nethers told me. "Every county official we spoke with emphasized how dangerous a situation this was."

Jack Hanna, TV celebrity, animal advocate, and former director of the Columbus Zoo, was there, and he backed up the actions the sheriff was taking. "There was no other way to handle this situation," Hanna said, according to the *Zanesville Times Recorder*. "Wild animals can be trained, not tamed. The public's safety was the most important thing in this situation."

As if the deputies didn't have enough problems on their hands, they also had to deal with looting. They stopped a jeep near the entrance to the Thompson property and discovered five local young men trying to make off with the body of a dead African lion that had been shot earlier by deputies. It's unclear just what the young men planned to do with the dead lion. The five were arrested, and the body of the lion was confiscated by police.

Sheriff Lutz eventually ordered all of the dead animal bodies to be collected and moved to a site near the Thompson Home.

He did this for two reasons: First, to get the dead animals away from public view. Second, and more importantly, to get an accurate count so they could then determine how many animals were still at large.

Sheriff Lutz told me that someone—it is not clear just who, but it was not a member of the sheriff's department—took a photo of all the dead animals laid side by side, row after row, species by species. That scene, when published, sickened animal lovers the world over. There were eighteen Bengal tigers, seventeen lions, six black bears, two grizzly bears, three cougars, one Macaque monkey, and one baboon. A total of forty-eight animals had been shot.

One human—Terry Thompson—was dead. No other humans had been injured.

At a press conference, Jack Hanna agreed the sheriff had made the right call. "It's a sad, sad situation and a very unnecessary one, but one that had to be dealt with," he said. "I think the public would be a lot more upset if children were attacked by a 300-pound tiger than the tiger having to be shot. This could have been a complete disaster, and the sheriff's office did their duty."

After two days it was over. State agriculture officials decided that the few remaining exotic animals—including three leopards still locked in cages, a baby grizzly bear, and two Macaque monkeys in cages inside the house—would be sent to the Columbus Zoo for a six-month quarantine and a health check.

According to GQ Magazine, Marion Thompson, Terry's widow, arrived on the scene and begged Jack Hanna and zoo officials not to take her "babies." She insisted on removing the two monkeys from their cage rather than allow zoo personnel to do so.

Terry Thompson left no note to explain why he decided to cut open the cages and release the animals. His body was sent to

Famed wildlife expert Jack Hanna of the Columbus Zoo joined Muskingum County sheriff Matt Lutz at a press conference. Hanna supported Lutz's order to shoot and kill the animals that were running loose. "There was no other way to handle this situation," Hanna said. "Wild animals can be trained, not tamed. The public's safety was the most important thing in this situation." *(Reuters / Alamy Stock Photo)*

the Licking County Coroner's Office for an autopsy. The coroner ruled that he died from a "self-inflicted gunshot to the head." The coroner also found a large bite wound to the head, consistent with a big cat's bite, that he said probably occurred just moments after Thompson's death.

The sheriff, in conjunction with state agricultural officials and Marion Thompson, decided to bury the animals. Marion Thompson reportedly picked a spot near the barns where a wide and 30-foot-deep hole was dug with excavating equipment, and the forty-eight animals were buried there.

Afterward . . .

As of this writing, Marion Thompson has never spoken publicly about the incident. She had a lengthy legal battle with the

Sam Kopchak, next-door neighbor of the Terry Thompson farm, was leading his horse, Red, in from the pasture when he found himself face-to-face with a full-grown male African lion. *(Courtesy of Tammy Satterfield)*

Ohio Agriculture Department about the removal of the living animals to the Columbus Zoo.

In January of 2012, the *Akron Beacon-Journal* reported that the jaguar that had been rescued from the Thompson farm, one of the six animals found in its cage after the shooting, had to be euthanized at the Columbus Zoo. According to zoo officials, the animal was struck on his neck as a cage door fell on him while attendants were doing routine feeding and cleaning. The animal had suddenly and unexpectedly darted back as the door was being shut. Zoo attendants gave the jaguar resuscitation, but it was unable to breath on its own, so a veterinarian made the decision to euthanize the animal.

On May 12, 2012, the Ohio Department of Agriculture director lifted the quarantine that had been issued on animals brought to the Columbus Zoo. According to the Associated Press, Marion Thompson, driving a pickup truck pulling a horse trailer, arrived at the Columbus Zoo and reclaimed the surviving five animals: a bear, two leopards, and two primates. She ignored reporters' questions and reportedly returned the animals to her farm near Zanesville.

In August 2013, Marion Thompson held an auction at the Zanesville farm. According to NBC News, the auction included Terry Thompson's collection of old cars and motorcycles as well as thirty horses, ponies, and donkeys. The person in charge of the auction, Jeff Koehler, told NBC News that the sale was to help Marion Thompson start the next chapter of her life. "As time goes on, we have to have endings," he said. "Marion knows it's time to sell a lot of these things and move on with her life."

According to the *Columbus Dispatch*, in February of 2014 Marian Thompson sent a letter to the Ohio Agriculture Department stating that she had relocated the surviving animals to other farms in Ohio. In the letter she wrote, "After two years of constant consideration and emotional turmoil, it is with deep sorrow that I inform you of the rehoming of my exotic animals. Their safety and well-being have always been my top priority and due to continual threats made towards them and the property upon which they reside I'm forced to make this decision."

What of Sam Kopchak, the man who first discovered the animal escape? The day before Marion Thompson's 2013 auction, Sam bought one of the horses he had seen running from that bear in the Thompson's pasture. Joe, a pinto, now lives with Sam's other horse, Red, in the barn on Kopchak Road.

The Thompson farm was sold, and Marion Thompson moved out. The roar of the animals has been replaced by the roar of motorcycles: The Thompson property is now a Motocross Track.

Acknowledgements

THIS BOOK COULD not have been written without the assistance of many people. I thank each and every one for your support in so many ways. I want to make a special note about the patience and assistance that I received from reference librarians throughout the state. Those responsible for this book are:

My wife, Bonnie, who became my eyes and typist

Bob Coy

Casey Coy

George Kilburg, pilot

Cindy Ruic

Dan Angelo

Pat Brady

Capt. Chris Zurcher, retired OSHP

Capt. Harv Callahan, retired OSHP

John Drago

Mark Thomas

Claire Glendenning

Ray Goll

The Women's International Air and Space Museum

Liberty Aviation Museum

Erie County Library, Sandusky, Ohio

Huron County Library, Huron, Ohio

Rondal Akers, M.D.

Ruth Fout

Barb Miller, Historian, OSHP

Gallia County Historical Society

Point Pleasant Museum and Learning Center

Bossard Memorial Library, Gallipolis, Ohio

Andre Bernier

John London, WLWT-TV, Cincinnati, Ohio

Virgil Dominic

Joe Tegreene

Mary Ellen Withrow

Scott Spears, WWGH radio, Marion, Ohio

Cleveland Public Library

Clermont County Public Library

Franklin County Public Library

Summit County Library

Lake County Library

Melanie Presler, Amherst Public Library

A.J. Colby

James Debevec

Gary and Bobbie Taylor

Cathy Wilson

Vicki and Terry Payer

Sheriff Gene Fisher

Daniel Hon

Kenneth (K.O.) Martin

Greene County Public Library

Dayton Metro Library

Greene County Historical Society

Elaine French

Fire Chief Dave Seidel

Chris Mills, branch manager, Huron
County Community Library

Tom Neel, New London Historical
Museum

Henry Timman, historian

Lynne Zele

Cleveland Police Museum

Western Reserve Fire Museum

Indian Museum of Lake County

Cleveland Museum of Natural History

Sam Kopchak

Tammy Sattersfield

Sheriff Matt Lutz, Muskingum County

Christa Luttmann, North West Regional
Liaison for Ohio Governor Mike
Dewine

Dave Nethers, WJW-TV

John McIntire, Muskingum County Public
Library

Guernsey County Library

(Lil) John Rinaldi

Scott Sabol

Al Baldie, retired lieutenant, Lorain Fire
Department

Tony Volak, retired assistant fire chief,
Lorain Fire Department

Ben Norton

Tom Brown

Lorain Public Library

Lorain Historical Society

Lorain County Historical Society

National Museum of the Great Lakes
(Toledo)

Mike Simkin

Jeff Hirsh

Fred Wittenbaum

Norma Rashid, Cincinnati TV personality

Peter and Melissa Luttmann

Bruce Bishop

Robert Corbett

Hamilton County Library

Butler County Library

Jeff Sigsworth

SFC Joshua Mann, Ohio adjutant general-
al's office

Linda Cuckovich

Anastasia Pantsios

David Gray, my publisher

Sources

Parachute Disaster on Lake Erie

Dreyer v. United States, 349F, Supp. 296 (N.D. Ohio 1972), US District Court for the Northern District of Ohio.
Robert Coy, interview in 2020
The Plain Dealer
Elyria Chronicle-Telegram
Sandusky Register
Liberty Aviation Museum, Port Clinton, Ohio
Dropzone.com, November 28, 2006

The Fitchville Nursing Home Fire

Elaine French, interview for this book
The Plain Dealer
Norwalk *Reflector-Herald*
Dave Seidel, current fire chief of Tri-Community (Greenwich) Fire Department (who was a young fireman at the scene), interview for this book
Elyria Chronicle-Telegram
Fireland, a documentary by Justin Zimmerman, 2006
Sandusky Register
The Mansfield News Journal

The Xenia Tornado

A.J. Colby, WJW-TV meteorologist, interview for this book
James Debevec, retired Ohio State Highway Patrol sergeant, interview for this book
Gary Taylor (retired staff lieutenant, Ohio State Highway Patrol) and Bobbie Taylor, interview for this book
Cathy Wilson, survivor of the Xenia tornado and, today, director of the Greene County Historical Society, interview for this book

Greene County Historical Society
Vicki and Terry Payer, interview for this book
Columbus Dispatch
Xenia Daily Gazette
Gene Fisher, sheriff of Greene County, interview for this book
Daniel Hon, former Ohio State Highway patrol officer, interview for this book
The Plain Dealer
Kenneth (K.O.) Martin, retired Ohio State Highway patrol, interview for this book
Barb Miller, historian, Ohio State Highway Patrol

The Blizzard of '78

Andre Bernier, WJW-TV meteorologist, interview for this book
Cincinnati Enquirer
John London, WLWT-TV, Cincinnati, interview for this book
The Plain Dealer
Toledo Blade
Virgil Dominic, former WJW-TV news director, interview for this book
Joseph Tegreene, former finance director for the city of Cleveland, interview for this book
The Sandusky Register
Mary Ellen Withrow, 40th treasurer of the United States, interview for this book
Gary Taylor, retired Ohio State Highway patrol officer, interview for this book
Columbus Dispatch
Youngstown Vindicator
Elyria Chronicle-Telegram
Dayton Daily News
The Marietta Times
Barb Miller, historian, Ohio State Highway Patrol

The Silver Bridge Disaster

The Silver Bridge Disaster of 1967 by Stephen G. Bullard, Bridget Gromek, Ruth Fout, and Martha Fout
The Plain Dealer
Gallipolis Daily Tribune
Ruth Fout, interview for this book
Huntington (W.V.) *Herald-Dispatch*
Point Pleasant River Museum and Learning Center
Dr. Rondal Akers, M.D., former news reporter for WCMI, Huntington, West Virginia; interview for this book
Cincinnati Enquirer

Gallia County Historical Society
Report on Silver Bridge Disaster by West Virginia Department of Transportation
Barb Miller, historian, Ohio State Highway Patrol

The Cleveland Circus Fire

Andre Bernier, WJW-TV meteorologist, interview for this book
The Cleveland Press
The Plain Dealer
The Call and Post
The New York Times
Western Reserve Fire Museum
Cleveland Police Museum
Indian Museum of Lake County
The News-Herald
Mansfield News Journal
Pittsburgh Post-Gazette
Cleveland Museum of Natural History

The Great Cleveland Balloon Launch Fiasco

WJW-TV video of the balloon launch
The Plain Dealer
Scott Sabol, WJW-TV meteorologist, interview for this book
Treb Heining, balloon promoter, interview with WJW-TV at the time of launch
Medina Gazette
John Rinaldi, WJW-TV personality, interview for this book
Guiness Book of World Records

The Roger Blough Inferno

Elyria Chronicle-Telegram
The Plain Dealer
The Lorain Journal
Lorain Historical Society
Al Baldie, retired lieutenant, Lorain Fire Department, interview for this book
Tony Volak, retired Lorain firefighter, interview for this book
National Museum of the Great Lakes (Toledo)
WBAY-TV Sturgeon Bay, Wisconsin

The Who Concert Stampede in Cincinnati

Mike Simkin, interview for this book
"The WHO Concert, The Night that Changed Rock," WCPO-TV documentary, December 2019
Cincinnati Enquirer
The New York Times
The Plain Dealer
Columbus Dispatch
Rolling Stone magazine
Jeff Hirsh, retired Cincinnati TV reporter, interview for this book
Dayton Daily News
Associated Press
Buffalo News
Fred Wittenbaum, interview for this book
P.E.M. Memorial Committee, Finneytown High School

The Zanesville Exotic Animal Escape

Sam Kopchak, interview for this book
Matt Lutz, sheriff of Muskingum County, interview for this book
"The Crazy True Story of the Zanesville Zoo Escape" by Chris Heath, *GQ Magazine*, 2012
Dave Nethers, WJW-TV reporter who covered this story, interview for this book
Columbus Dispatch
The Zanesville Times Recorder
Akron Beacon Journal
Associated Press
NBC news

About the Author

NEIL ZURCHER IS a retired television journalist. He began his career in 1954 at the *Oberlin News-Tribune* in Oberlin, Ohio, then switched to radio reporting in 1961 at WEOL Radio in Elyria, Ohio. While working in radio he also became a free-lance reporter for WJW-TV in Cleveland, and he became their first full-time street reporter in 1967. He was associated with WJW-TV for more than fifty years, retiring in 2017.

Zurcher is today best known for his long-running travel series "One Tank Trips." He was the original host and produced the show for more than thirty years. Former Ohio governor George Voinovich called him "one of the most respected and knowledgeable travel writers in the state."

But his earlier work in news reporting during the 1950s through 1970s was varied and widely recognized. He reported on major stories, including riots and civil unrest. He was on the scene in 1968 when the Ohio National Guard stormed the Ohio Penitentiary to rescue guards who had been taken hostage. In 1969, a television documentary he wrote and produced exposing the crumbling condition of a county orphanage was nominated for an Emmy award. In 1970 he wrote and produced a documentary exposing the adverse effects of strip-mining on the Ohio landscape. In 1971, a mini-documentary he wrote and produced about U.S. prisoners of war in southeast Asia won an

Emmy award from the National Academy of Television Arts and Sciences.

The National Society of Professional Journalists gave Zurcher their Distinguished Service Award in 1999. He was honored by the National Academy of Television Arts and Sciences with a rare Gold Circle Award for his fifty years in television in 2013. He received the coveted Award for Excellence in Broadcasting from the Cleveland Association of Broadcasters. He was inducted into The Cleveland Press Club Hall of Fame. He was inducted into the Ohio Broadcasters Hall of Fame and received their "Living Legacy" award in 2007.

Zurcher is the author of several books about Ohio, including *The Best of One Tank Trips*, *Ohio Oddities*, *Strange Tales From Ohio*, and the memoir *Tales from the Road*.

He is married to his wife, Bonnie, and has three children, four grandchildren, and one great-grandchild.

Other books of interest . . .

Strange Tales from Ohio
True Stories of Remarkable People, Places, and Events in Ohio History

Neil Zurcher

Ohio history can get pretty strange! Meet Ashtabula's famed Headless Chicken, who lived without his noggin for 38 days. Was Ohio really bombed by the Japanese in WWII? Introducing the inventor of disposable diapers . . . For anyone who enjoys history with a twist, here are 75 tales of the Buckeye State's most unusual people, places, and events.

"A delightful read . . . Zurcher chooses his anecdotes well, balancing scandalous murder mysteries and the truly odd with lighter fare about Ohio's famous inventors and funniest first achievements." – Akron Life Magazine

Ohio Oddities
A Guide to the Curious Attractions of the Buckeye State

Neil Zurcher

The Buckeye State has no shortage of strange, silly, goofy, quirky, eccentric, and just plain weird places, people, and things—if you know where to look. Discover the World's Largest Cuckoo Clock, the nation's only vacuum cleaner museum, Balto the Wonder Dog, the "bottomless" Blue Hole of Casalia, and lots more hard-to-believe stuff!

"Oddly delightful . . . From the Blue Hole to the headless chicken, it's a wonderfully wacky page turner." – Martin Savidge, CNN

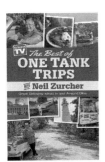

The Best of One Tank Trips
Great Getaway Idea In and Around Ohio

Neil Zurcher

Discover the best and most unusual getaway ideas in and around Ohio! Popular TV travel reporter Neil Zurcher has driven more than a million miles to find fun and offbeat attractions, including quirky museums, one-of-a-kind restaurants, natural wonders, historic villages, and more—just a short drive from home! Here are his all-time favorites. eyes. Filled with fun details.

More at **www.grayco.com**

Other books of interest . . .

Tales from the Road
Memoirs from a Lifetime of Ohio Travel, Television, and More

Neil Zurcher

After a million miles and four decades as a TV reporter, Neil Zurcher has many great stories to tell: He met Prince Charles in a bathroom, and tripped and fell on President Gerald Ford. He raced on an elephant, piloted a glider, and hung from a trapeze. He survived a hotel fire, a tornado, and countless stunts for the camera. Fun tales well told.

"A sparkling gem of a book . . . Intermingled with the pratfalls, hijinks and practical jokes are bittersweet stories of love and romance, tragedy and triumph . . . a remarkably well-written book." – The Morning Journal

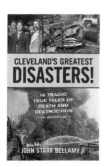

Cleveland's Greatest Disasters!
Sixteen Tragic Tales of Death and Destruction: An Anthology

John Stark Bellamy II

An anthology of the 15 best true Cleveland disaster stories from Bellamy's popular book series, including the apocalyptic East Ohio Gas Company explosion of 1944, the unspeakably horrible 1908 Collinwood School fire, the Ashtabula Bridge Disaster, and the oddly named yet quite ghastly Doodlebug Disaster. Includes 65 photos.

It Came From Ohio
True Tales of the Weird, Wild, and Unexplained

James Renner

An investigative reporter looks into 13 tales of mysterious, creepy, and unexplained events in the Buckeye State. Includes the giant, spark-emitting Loveland Frog; the bloodthirsty Melon Heads of Kirtland; the lumber-wielding Werewolf of Defiance; the Mothman of the Ohio River; the UFO that inspired "Close Encounters of the Third Kind"; and more.

More at **www.grayco.com**